Tips and Traps
When Selling a Home

Other McGraw-Hill Books by Robert Irwin

The McGraw-Hill Real Estate Handbook (1984)
The Handbook of Property Management (1986)
How to Find Hidden Real Estate Bargains (1986)
Making Mortgages Work for You (1987)
How to Find and Manage Profitable Properties (1988)
Tips and Traps When Buying a Home (1990)

Robert Irwin

Tips and Traps
When Selling
a Home

McGraw-Hill, Inc.
New York   San Francisco   Washington, D.C.   Auckland   Bogotá
Caracas   Lisbon   London   Madrid   Mexico City   Milan
Montreal   New Delhi   San Juan   Singapore
Sydney   Tokyo   Toronto

Library of Congress Cataloging-in-Publication Data

Irwin, Robert
  Tips and traps when selling a home/Robert Irwin.
  p. cm.
  ISBN 0-07-032137-X—ISBN 0-07-032139-6 (pbk.)
  1. House selling.   2. Real estate business.   I. Title.
HD1379.I674   1990
333.33'83—dc20   89-39203
                                                                          CIP

    4567890   DOC/DOC   9876543

ISBN 0-07-032137-X

ISBN 0-07-032139-6 {PBK.}

*The editors for this book were James Bessent and Jim Halston, the designer was
Naomi Auerbach, and the production supervisor was Suzanne W. Babeuf. This
book was set in Baskerville by the McGraw-Hill Publishing Company Professional & Reference Division composition unit.*

Printed and bound by R. R. Donnelley and Sons

*This book contains the author's opinions. Some material in this book
may be affected by changes in the law (or changes in interpretations
of the law) or changes in market conditions since the manuscript was
prepared. Therefore, the accuracy and completeness of the information
contained in this book and the opinions based on it cannot be guaranteed. Neither the author nor the publisher is engaged in rendering
investment, legal, tax, accounting, or other similar professional services. If these services are required, the reader should obtain them from
a competent professional. The publisher and author hereby specifically
disclaim any liability for loss incurred as a consequence of following
any advice or applying information presented in this book.*

 This book is printed on recycled, acid-free paper containing a minimum of 50% recycled de-
inked fiber.

Contents

Preface

This year nearly three million people will sell their personal residences, their homes. For many it will be a quick and painless procedure. For many more, however, it will be a time of frustration, anger, lost money and, perhaps, fear. Today, selling your home can be not only tricky but also fraught with perils.

Selling your home, learning about the new laws concerning disclosure, finding and dealing with a broker, with the buyer, the attorney, the escrow officer, carrying back financing, working out the tax problems, and, of course, reading and understanding the complex documents can be a confusing, difficult, if not frightening experience. Even though I have purchased and sold more houses than I care to remember, I still learn something new in every sale.

It was with this concern for sellers and the knowledge that in today's world, sellers are at a distinct disadvantage ("let the seller beware" is *today's* motto), that I undertook to write what I hope is a book filled with answers. I have tried to anticipate the landmines and the swift currents and prepare you, the seller, to deal successfully with these.

I've tried to put myself entirely in the position of a seller and see things as you see them. The advice is from your perspective. I've attempted to give you guidelines to follow and to warn you in advance of traps.

I hope you, the reader, will find this book enlightening as well as helpful and that it will allow you, with more ease and confidence, to sell your home quickly and at the price you want.

Robert Irwin

Introduction: The Real Trouble With Selling

In the old days, the most quoted maxim in selling real estate was, "caveat emptor," Latin for, "let the buyer beware." Today that's all changed. Today's slogan should read, "let the seller beware!"

Consumer protection laws and a high-priced market have turned the world of selling your home topsy turvy. In the old days all you had to worry about was finding a buyer. Today, you not only have to worry about finding a buyer, but you also must hope that your buyer won't turn around and try to rescind (void) the deal after the purchase because of something you said or didn't say or did or didn't do!

Today, selling a home not only means finding a great broker or doing a bang-up job of selling it yourself, it also means walking a fine line between promoting your property and disclosing all the faults it may have.

Of course, that doesn't mean that it's hard to sell. Nearly three million properties are sold each year. It just means that it's tricky and you need to know where the land mines are.

Dealing With The Problems

If you are thinking of selling your home, condo, or co-op, you are faced with some or all of these problems:

- Selling it yourself. (Do you really stand a chance?)
- Finding an agent who will work hard for you and produce buyers.

- Getting the price you want and feel you deserve.
- Negotiating to your advantage (not just giving away the cow with the milk).
- Fixing up the property so the buyers won't be able to come back at you later on.
- Legally avoiding paying taxes on the sale (if you can).

Finding a Buyer

The first problem is locating a buyer—obviously, no buyer, no sale. When you buy a stock or bond or commodity future, generally speaking you can be quite confident that you won't have any trouble at all selling. Indeed, to dispose of your investment, all that you need do is call up your securities broker and speak the magic word, "Sell!" Almost by the time you put down your phone, your stock or bond or commodity has been sold.

Real estate is different. While it is probably true that there is a buyer for every home, there may only be one buyer and that person may not know or even care that you're trying to sell. To put it another way, unlike other investments, real estate isn't really very liquid. When it's time to sell your home you may find that:

1. You may have to wait to find a buyer, sometimes for many months or in extreme cases, years.
2. It will cost you a great deal to sell, as much as ten percent or more of the sales price.
3. You may not be able to get what you consider to be the market price.

Answers to the problems of time, cost, and price are given in this book. You will learn how to attract serious buyers, how to avoid paying excess costs and, perhaps most important, how to get your fair price.

Preparing Your Property

In addition to finding a buyer, there's the matter of preparing your property. In the old days that meant a fresh coat of paint and some gardening work. Today that often involves hiring a house inspector to locate the bad plumbing, wiring, heating, and whatever and then spending a small fortune fixing it—quite a different proposition.

Today in most states you, in effect, have to warrant the condition of your house. Much like the manufacturer of a product, to a greater degree than ever before, you are responsible for what you sell, even after the sale!

This book presents solutions to handling the warranty problems. You'll learn where to save money when fixing up your property for sale. You'll discover items you must disclose to a buyer and what you don't have to say.

Handling Agents

Want to see a stampede? Just put a "For Sale By Owner" sign in your front yard. If you don't get 20 calls, visits, and solicitations by agents the first week (perhaps the first day!), you're living in a most unusual part of the country (or nobody can see your sign!).

Agents will pester you and until you sign on with one, they may even try to intimidate you. Of course, they know all the rules and procedures when selling a home and unless you are well versed in real estate, you don't know very much about it at all. You may feel you're at their mercy.

This book explains what you need to know in order to successfully sell your home. It also gives you valuable clues on handling those agents.

Who Should Read
This Book

In *Tips and Traps When Selling a Home* you will find solutions to all of the problems mentioned here and many more that you will have to face, but haven't even thought of yet. You'll get easy-to-understand explanations of the most complex rules and procedures. You'll learn what your best options are when hiring a broker or selling by yourself. You'll even find idea lists to help you plan ahead.

This book is for anyone who is selling their home (there are special sections for condo and co-op owners). It doesn't matter whether you just bought it and are struggling to get out without losing money or have owned it for years and are trying to conserve your appreciation. You'll find answers and decision making help here.

1
Fixing Up Your Home to Attract Buyers

You've decided to sell your home. It really doesn't matter why—maybe you've been transferred, or you want a bigger house, or perhaps you want to cash in on your equity. Regardless, once you've made the decision to sell, the next step is to evaluate your home—is it ready to sell? Or do you need to fix it up first?

The price that you ultimately get, indeed the salability of your home, depends to a large degree on the condition of your property. We'll look at other factors in determining price and salability in the next chapter.

Your Attitude Toward Fixing Up Your Home

There are two distinct attitudes when it comes to readying a home for sale. On the one hand are those who will repair and replace all those broken parts that they were perfectly content to live with while they owned the property, all in the hopes of getting a quick sale for top dollar. On the other hand are those who aren't willing to do a thing to fix up a house for sale. Instead, they simply put it on the market as is.

The important question for most home sellers, of course, is which attitude is correct? Which way yields the most money and the quickest sale?

The answer, like most answers in life, is—it depends. Whether or not it pays to expend some effort, a lot of effort, or no effort fixing up your home to sell depends on the following:

1. The market *when you sell*

2. The condition of your home

3. Your level of energy

The Market When You Sell

I live in California where the housing market is either hot or warm. Rarely, if ever, is it cool and never, ever is it cold. That's significant when it comes time to sell.

In a Hot Market

If the market is hot, it means that there are far more buyers looking than there are sellers offering. Houses are much in demand. You most certainly have heard of (or have even experienced) a hot market. Buyers wait in line for days just to get a chance to buy a new home. When you put your resale on the market, you immediately get three offers, two of which are for more than you're asking! Hot means hot.

Buyers in a hot market are very frequently more than willing to overlook a few maintenance problems. In some cases they're willing to overlook a whole lot of serious problems.

For example, a friend was recently going to put his home up for sale. The house was over 20 years old, and not much maintenance had been done to it. He told me he was determined to get top dollar. To assure that, he was going to paint the entire house, inside and out, put on a new roof, and relandscape the front yard. I started to object, but he said his mind was made up. When he was finished, he would put the house on the market for top dollar, which he figured would be $200,000. (See the next chapter for information on determining the right price.)

One day I went over to see him, and there he was up on a ladder, painting away. The roofers had just come and put on a very nice looking new roof, to the tune of $7000. "Almost done," he said. "Just a few weeks more of work."

While we were talking, I noticed that his next door neighbor had placed a "For Sale By Owner" sign in his front yard. The neighbor's tract house was a duplicate of my friend's except that the neighbor hadn't done a thing to fix up his property. No painting, no new roof, no landscaping. The house didn't look terrible, but it was far from being in great shape.

That night I got a call from my friend. He was enraged. "Can you imagine?" he asked. "My neighbor just sold his house, without fixing it up a bit…for $200,000! Can you imagine?"

The upshot of this true story is that my friend finished his fix up work and then put his property on the market and eventually sold it for $210,000. However, when the roofing and painting and yardwork were tallied up, they amounted to almost $10,000, meaning that the time and money he spent fixing up were really wasted. Chances are he could have sold it with no effort for $200,000, given the hot market he was in.

Tip

In a hot market, buyers tend to overlook a lot about a house's condition. Yes, if it's in terrible shape, they will either not buy or knock the price down. But if it's in "okay" shape, chance's are they won't complain. In a hot market, it's hard enough just finding a house to buy in a price range a buyer can afford, let alone worrying about the small stuff.

In a Warm Market

Things change pretty dramatically when we move from a hot market to a warm market. In a warm market, there are a lot of buyers and a lot of sellers. Buyers don't feel compelled to rush in and make offers. On the other hand, sellers aren't worried that it's going to take six months to sell a property either. In a warm market, it typically takes one to three months to sell a home.

In a warm market, buyers take their time finding just the right home for them. If they find two homes that they like, all other factors such as location being equal, they'll select the one that's in the best condition.

If a house is run-down, not terrible, but about the same as in our example for a hot market, a buyer may simply pass and find a similar house in better shape.

Thus, in a warm market for you as a seller, fixing up your home prior to sale means two things—you're likely to get a better price and, what can be even more important, you're likely to sell much faster.

Trap

Many sellers fall into the trap of thinking that by doing excessive fix-up work to their house, they can make even more money on the sale. Chances are that just isn't so. Your property will have a top market value beyond which it just won't go at the present time. What you do when you fix it up is to try to present it in such way as to get that top dollar. You do the *minimal amount of fix-up possible.* Any additional fixing is just icing on the cake—it costs you more money and time without returning a significantly higher price.

In a Cool or Cold Market

A cool market is where there are many houses for sale and few buyers. As a result, housing prices are dropping. A cold market is where there are *no* buyers. A cold market seldom occurs.

Cool markets occurred in the northeast and southwest in the late 1980s. A cold market occurred in parts of Texas and Oklahoma when oil prices collapsed and in the Midwest when agricultural prices collapsed in the mid-1980s. In a cold market, it makes no sense to fix up a property, since no matter what you do it won't sell. In a cool market, however, that's not necessarily the case.

Phoenix, for example, had a cool market right into 1990. The reason was overbuilding. Although the area had strong growth and a steady influx of new people, builders went wild building on every patch of bare land—which in Phoenix seemed endless.

I have a friend in Phoenix who tried to sell her house in early 1989 and was told that it would take about six to eight *months* to find a buyer. She wondered if fixing it up could shorten that period and return a higher price?

The answer was yes and no. Fixing it up would definitely help. However, unlike being in a hot or even warm market, in a cool market you cannot expect to get back out everything you put in when fixing up a property.

Thus my friend had to be judicious about what she did. A coat of paint inside and out, with her doing the work, cost less than $500 and helped enormously. A new roof, which the house needed, however, would have cost $7000. She considered doing it, but decided she'd only be able to raise the price of the house by $3500 if the roof was put on—half of what it would cost. On the other hand, she figured that by lowering the price $3500, she could entice a prospective buyer to purchase. Lowering the price and *not doing the work* saved her half the cost of a new roof when she put the house on the market.

In a cool market, you have to very, very careful. Most work you put into fix-up won't help that much. On the other hand, not fixing up the property at all might mean that you'd have to wait much longer, and accept a lower price. In many cases it may be easier, quicker, and ultimately more profitable to simply start with a lower price.

The Condition of Your Home

Having said that market conditions should be the biggest influence on whether or not you should fix up your home before you sell, let's turn to the next most important consideration... the condition of the home itself. Let's divide homes into three categories:

Those in pretty good shape

Those needing obvious fix-up work

Real dogs

Homes in Pretty Good Shape

If your home is in pretty good shape, you probably can get by with little to no major fix-up work. Pretty good shape means:

The paint isn't too bad on the outside (no blisters, peeling, or fading) or inside (no marks or scratches).

The lawns don't have bald spots and aren't overgrown with weeds and that the house has hedges and trees and decent landscaping.

All the appliances work.

If your house is in pretty good shape, what you should do, however, is launch a *major clean-up effort.* If you've lived in your present home for more than six months, chances are you've got a couple of loads of trash and throwaways stashed here and there.

Tip

Buyers like to see themselves in a house. They like to see where they would put their furniture, make their meals, sleep, and relax. They need some furniture and items in the home to get the "feel of it." But if it's cluttered with your stuff, they will have trouble seeing themselves in your home. A good rule of thumb is to clear out all of the rooms of everything but the basics. Throw it out, store it, give it away, or do whatever you need to get rid of it. Leaving it around will slow down the sale and may cut back the price you are offered.

Here are lists of items get to rid of or to clean up before you put the house up for sale.

Get rid of:

1. Extra furniture. One double/queen/king or two twin beds in a bed-room is maximum. One table and set of chairs in a dining room. No cluttered chairs or couches in living or family room. No rugs on top of rugs. Try storing the extra stuff with friends or relatives.

2. Clothes that are not in drawers or *neatly* hung in closets.

3. Toys scattered on the floor.

4. Any items that would get in the way of a buyer's appreciation of the house.

Tip
_____

Visit a model home at a nearby tract of new houses. See firsthand the relatively few items they put in the houses. Get ideas there for your home.

Clean up:

1. The kitchen. *Never, never* leave dirty dishes out when showing a house. Nothing turns buyers off more than this.

2. The carpets. The first thing that buyers look at are the carpets. Clean carpets make a positive impression.

3. The drapes. They're the next thing that buyers look at.

4. Smudges or spots on walls. Most can be wiped off with detergent and a sponge.

5. Junk and trash in the front, back, or side yards. Haul it away. You're going to have to move it as soon as you sell, anyhow.

6. The front door. Repaint it. It only takes a few minutes and a pint of paint, yet it's the first thing that buyers see. Remember about first impressions?

7. Windows. Buyers like to be able to see out. Clean or replace old screens too.

These are things you can do if your home is already in pretty good shape. Now, let's consider a home in not so good shape. A list of major repair items appears below. Presumably, your home does not need *all* of these. But even one is a major cost repair.

A Home Needing Major Fix-Up

You have to make the decision "if it's worth it" depending on the market. While the work needed to be done will differ from house to house, in all cases you will need to do at least one major project. The following list describes the most common major fix-ups as well as tips on how to handle them.

1. Roof—Sometimes you can simply fix an old roof where it's leaking and not replace it. The cost is far, far less.

2. Insulation—Older homes did not have much insulation, but today, in some jurisdictions, you must bring your home up to a minimum code standard in order to sell. In an attic space, the cost for adding blown-in insulation is fairly low. To add insulation to walls on an already constructed house, however, is enormously costly and should be avoided if at all possible.

3. Electrical and plumbing—You'll need to bring these up to safety standards in any event. In most cases the work needed to be done is minimal. On the other hand, if you have to convert galvanized steel pipes to copper pipes, be prepared for a major blow to your wallet.

4. Walls—External stucco should be patched, unless it's so badly broken up that it has to be totally replaced. Patching is cheap; replacement is very expensive. Interior wallboard should be patched where there are holes. You can do this yourself for next to nothing.

5. Garage door—New hinges are a good idea for safety reasons and are inexpensive. Most wooden doors can be repaired inexpensively. Metal doors may have to be replaced.

6. Landscaping—If you put in a new lawn by sod, it costs more, but is instantly green. Seeds take up to three months to produce lush grass. Forget about adding shade trees—they need years to grow and planting already large trees is costly. Flower beds, however, are inexpensive and add color and vitality to landscaping. Also, fix the fence if it's falling down. Buyers start adding up costs when they see a broken fence.

7. Appliances—In most cases they must be fixed or replaced. Sometimes it's cheaper to replace than to fix. For example, an entire electric range and oven may cost under $400, while a single burner (there are usually five to seven on the unit, including oven) could cost $100.

There could, of course, be other areas requiring major repair. In all cases you should get bids as well as competitively price materials yourself to weigh the cost of the repair against whether or not you'll get your money out from the sale and/or whether or not it will help you sell faster, given the market conditions.

A Real Dog

Many people have never seen a house in this condition. Typically it results from absentee owners who rent the place out to tenants who just don't care. For many readers the following list will just make you feel good about your own property. Things that could be wrong with the property and that would make your hair stand on end could include:

Appliances—ripped apart, stolen or smashed

Bathroom fixtures—ripped off walls or out of floors and broken

Light fixtures—stolen, smashed (including the electrical receptacle)

Windows—broken

Doors—broken or missing

Screens—gone

Plumbing—broken lines

Electrical—main circuit box smashed, circuit breakers broken, wiring pulled out

Walls and ceiling—major holes

Yard—no landscaping, weeds, rocks, and dirt

Fence—broken

Exterior—stucco falling apart, wood torn off or scratched, metal siding bent or broken loose

"Ridiculous," you may say. "A house could never get that bad." I've seen them that bad and worse. But being in terrible shape doesn't mean the house is valueless. In all but a cold market, homes always have some value. The condition just means that you have to decide on a plan of action. You have several choices.

1. Fix it up completely.

2. Fix it up for safety and cosmetic effect.

3. Let it alone and sell for much less.

A Lack of Imagination

At this point you have to realize that buyers ordinarily suffer from an appalling lack of imagination. If you have a house that is a real dog and you're fortunate enough to get a buyer to walk into the front door, chances are 99 out of 100 the buyer will immediately turn around and walk out. The vast majority of buyers, even investor-buyers, won't want to fool around with a real dog *even if the price is cut-rate.*

That means that in order to sell the property you're probably going to have to do some work. Either you fix it up totally or just cosmetically enough to sell.

Tip

It's going to cost big bucks to fix up a real dog of a house. You may need to get short-term financing in the form of a home-owner's loan or a home-equity loan. In many cases the interest on these is tax deductible as are *many* of your fix-up expenses. (See later chapters on tax solutions and financing.)

I would suggest a *total* fix-up of a "dog" only if you're in a high value area and if you have sufficient equity. In such an area, the complete fix-up can often be justified by a bumped-up price on resale. In a modest priced area, however, the difference of what you can get for a cosmetic fix-up versus a total fix-up probably does not warrant the more expensive approach. For example, if it costs $30,000 to totally fix up the property and the total fix-up will result in a price increase of only $10,000, it obviously isn't worth the total effort. A cosmetic fix-up might result in a sales price of $60,000, whereas a total fix-up might result in a sales price of only $70,000.

On the other hand if the total fix-up still costs $30,000, but the house sells for $300,000 for a cosmetic fix-up and $350,000 with a total fix-up, the total approach makes sense because of the $50,000 price bump-up. Note in both houses the difference between prices is *the same percentage.*

Trap

Cosmetic does not mean leaving health and safety problems undone. In order to sell in most areas of the country today, the house must be up to at least minimal building and safety standards.

Evaluating Your Level of Energy

Finally there is the matter of how much energy you are willing (or have) to devote to the fix-up. Some of us are natural putterers, fixing up a place is fun for us.

Then, there are the rest of us, probably a majority, who have two left hands and who wouldn't think of trying to do fix-up ourselves. We'd hire it out, and then we'd hate the inconvenience of laborers and materials coming in and out. The hassle, noise, and so forth would make it unbearable.

Here's my suggestion. If you don't want to (or can't) spend a lot of energy fixing up your home before you sell, forget it. Take the lower price. Wait the longer time to find a buyer.

For you, the lower price and longer sales period may be worthwhile. For you, it may be better to just avoid all the hassle and wear and tear and just let the property go as is.

Sometimes it's more important to cater to yourself than to cater to your house.

On the other hand, if you're a bundle of energy, then by all means leap into the fray and fix up your house—depending, of course, on its condition and the market. Try to do as much of the work yourself as that's actually the best way to save money.

2

Pricing Your Property to Sell

If you want to attract buyers to your home like bees to honey, you need to price it attractively. Favorable terms, an appealing appearance, and good location are all factors that will attract buyers. But nothing speaks louder than price.

On the other hand, you don't want to give your home away. The price you ultimately select must be low enough to cause a buyer to want to make an offer, yet be high enough to give you your full money's worth. How do you arrive at the correct price?

Tip

Never get locked into a price. Your initial judgment may be wrong. You may price the house too high or too low. Be prepared to lower or to raise your price as conditions change.

Seeing It From the Buyer's Perspective

Many books written on real estate suggest that you get an appraisal to determine your home's value. Call in a registered appraiser or a competent real estate agent and they'll quickly tell you what the house will bring on the open market. That's not a bad idea, and their judgment is usually pretty close, but calling them in isn't always satisfying. How do you know they're correct? Maybe this is the one time that they mess up and give you a lowball figure, and you end up selling your home for too little? It could happen.

Ultimately, you're the one who has to be fully convinced of the true value, the right price for your home. Having someone come in and tell you isn't necessarily going to convince you. Only when you truly believe for yourself are you going to be satisfied that you have the right price.

The best way to begin believing in the price is to see your home from the buyer's perspective. This isn't hard, but it does take a considerable bit of honesty. Look at your home as a buyer does, and you'll quickly recognize whether an appraiser or a broker is giving you the true value.

It isn't hard to imagine what buyers look for. Actually there are three main factors that determine price, and they are usually in the following order:

Neighborhood

Age

Condition

Neighborhood

Buyers don't buy houses, they buy neighborhoods. Honestly now, if you were going out to buy a house, would you buy your current neighborhood? Or would you look at a newer, nicer, neighborhood?

If you feel that your neighborhood is top notch, ask yourself if you're being totally honest. Remember, buyers "look" at a neighborhood. They don't know that Mrs. Green across the street is the most wonderful person in the world and the Browns down the block will lend you any tool or that Henry Smith next door has wonderful children who make the best baby-sitters.

The buyers don't know the friends you've made. Instead, they look at these things:

1. The desirability of the neighborhood in terms of community perceptions. ("Oh, you live in Meadow Brook, everyone wants to live there." or, "Oh, you live in Cedar Hollow, how sad for you.")

2. The condition of neighborhood homes and landscaping.

3. The size of the homes in the neighborhood (beds and baths—are there likely to be large families living there or small).

4. Closeness to shopping, schools, libraries, hospital, fire department.

5. The availability of police protection. (A gated community is considered the ultimate here.)

Notice this—of the five biggest concerns of buyers, none are under your direct control. You can't control your home's location, the neighborhood, the size of homes in the area, proximity to shopping, or whether you're in a gated community.

In other words, most of what will attract a buyer to your home is external. Now, take a moment to reevaluate. Just how good is your neighborhood, really?

Neighborhood Evaluation Checklist

1. Community perceptions?

Good [ ]
Bad [ ]
Indifferent [ ]

2. Neighborhood condition?

Good [ ]
Medium [ ]
Bad [ ]

3. Size of neighborhood homes?

Large [ ]
Medium [ ]
Small [ ]

4. Closeness to shopping, schools, libraries, hospital, fire department?

Nearby [ ]
Driving distance [ ]
Far [ ]

5. Security?

Good [ ]
Bad [ ]

Age

Another big factor is the age of your home. In general, buyers like newer homes, because they have fewer maintenance problems and more modern conveniences, or very old homes, probably because they are supposed to be colorful and have charming features. Houses between 7 and 40 or 50 years of age are considered in-between. Buyers know they're going to have some maintenance problems and there isn't going to be that charm.

How old is *your* home? If you don't know, go into a bathroom and lift up the top of the toilet tank (not the seat, the tank top). Turn it over. Almost always, stamped into the porcelain is a date. That's when the tank top was built and is probably pretty close to the date your home was built, unless someone has more recently replaced the tank top. You can quickly calculate the age of your home.

	YES	NO
Do you have a home less than seven years old?	[ ]	[ ]
Do you have an older, charming home?	[ ]	[ ]

Condition

In the previous chapter we considered how to improve your home's condition. It's an important consideration; however, keep in mind that it's usually third on the list for buyers after neighborhood and age.

Yet, since it's the only thing that we really have any control over, most of us do make a big effort to get our home into shape before we sell. Many times we fix and improve things that we had been content to live with.

Now, try again to be as honest as possible. Given your home's:

1. Neighborhood

2. Age

3. Condition

How much do you really think it's worth?

Getting to Know the Market

If you're still not sure, it's probably because you aren't familiar with the current housing market in your area. Just because you live in Nashville, for example, is no reason for you to have any detailed knowledge of the Nashville housing market.

Yes, you may have some idea from recent sales of what houses are selling for in your neighborhood, but that's not exactly scientific. You need to get a good handle on competitive housing prices.

How do you learn about the housing market? The first thing to do is to contact a real estate broker.

Using a Broker's Knowledge

No, I'm not suggesting you *list* your house with the agent, just that you contact one for information. In almost every case, the agent will be more than willing to give it to you in the hopes that you'll eventually list with that agent.

Here's what you tell the agent:

"I'm thinking of putting my house up for sale. I want to ask a competitive price. Can you supply me with a list of *comparables* for my home?"

What you are asking for is a list of homes that have recently sold and the sales prices and original listing prices that are similar to your home. Just compare this list with your home and you'll have a pretty good idea of the market.

Finding Comparables

The reason an agent can easily provide you with comparables is that almost all areas of the country have listing services (such as the Multiple Listing Service), and nearly all agents belong to them. Today these listing service groups are computerized, and they provide their members with lists of sales and houses currently for sale, going back months, sometimes even years. On most services, the agent, with the flick of a few buttons on a computer, can pull up sales and the original listing prices in your section of town, your neighborhood, even your street.

Think of the time this saves you. This information is readily available from an agent. If you were to try to discover it yourself, it could take you weeks of work. That's why I suggest that an agent should be your first stop. It's the quickest way to learn the market in your area.

When you get the list of comparables, first make sure the houses are indeed comparable. Check that they have the same number of bedrooms and baths, a pool (if you have one), and other amenities. Eliminate those houses that are dissimilar.

Next, if the list is fairly long, *throw out the highest-priced and lowest-priced sales.* Just assume those were flukes and won't be repeated.

Tip

Look for list prices of homes that were *recently sold.* Beware of looking at the price of houses currently on the market—they can be deceptive. Many of the homes currently listed either will post price reductions as the sellers get desperate or, if the house doesn't sell for a particularly high price, will be completely taken off the market. Just because a house has been listed with an agent doesn't mean it will be sold at the listed price. The number of houses which were listed but which didn't sell because the sellers got discouraged can be high. It largely depends on the condition of the market, but in an average warm market, it's probably close to 15 to 25 percent. In a cool market it can be 50 percent or higher. Looking at prices of houses currently listed, therefore, can give you a false sense of value.

Analyzing Comparables

Now, you've gotten your comparables list down to manageable size. Here's what to do with it. First, look for the percentage difference between the price sold and the listed price.

The Percentage Differential

1. Check sales prices going back no more than six months. These are current sales. Anything further back is suspect, as the market may have changed since the last sale.

2. Check listing prices of the homes that sold. For each sale, there's also a listing price, note it.

   Do this for at least six different homes.
   Now take your calculator and do a little math. Divide the *sales price into the listing price* for those half-dozen homes. This will give you the percentage difference between the asking (list) price and the sales price. It will tell you how active the market is as well as how much less than your asking price you can expect to sell your home for. It will tell you, in effect, the softness of the market. Here's a sample of how it's done:

Analyzing the Percentage Differential

Listing Price	Sales Price	Percentage Difference
113,000	110,000	−2.7
120,000	108,000	−10.0
115,000	106,000	−7.8
118,000	110,000	−6.8
112,000	109,000	−2.7
105,000	107,000	+1.9
114,000	108,000	−4.7 Average

The percentage difference is the softness of the market. It tells you a number of things including how realistic the asking prices are for homes in the area, how strong or weak the market is in terms of buyers paying the asking price, and indirectly, how long it may take to sell your home.

If the average percentage differences are between 0 and 5 percent, you're in a strong market. You can pretty much get what you're asking for your home, if your price is reasonable.

If the percentages are between 5 and 10 percent, you're in a soft market. You'd might be better off dropping your price initially and going for a quick sale.

If the percentages are between 10 and 20 percent, the market is very weak. Unless you're prepared to drop your price considerably, it may be a long time before you're able to get your price.

Twenty percent and above and the market is in trouble. No sale may be possible at this time.

Check the Time Lag

Another important factor is how long it takes to sell a home. Your agent can usually provide you with a list detailing the date the properties were listed and the date they were sold. You can quickly calculate the time it took between listing and sale of a particular home. Some areas offer an average time figure—the average time a listed house is on the market before a sale. The agent normally cannot provide you with a list which tells how long houses currently listed have been on the market. The reason is that a buyer could use this list to force down the price of a seller who has had a house on the market for a very long time. In most states giving the buyer such information would be considered unethical at the least.

Any time lag under two months for an average sale is considered a good market. Over three is a weak market. Over six months is a very bad market.

Look for the Average List and
Average Sales Price

The tendency when looking at a list of comparables is to say that the lower priced sales don't apply to you; the higher priced sales are what you can expect to get. This is a mistake. It's better to get an average of all sales prices and assume that your house falls close to it. To get an average of sales prices, add all the prices and divide by the number of examples, or simply ask your agent. The listing service may already provide an average sales price for recently sold homes in your area.

Do the same thing for the listing price. Find out the average listing price either by adding up the cases and then dividing by the number of cases or again, ask your agent. The agent may have that information readily available as well.

What Price Should You Ask for Your House?

Should you ask the average sales price, the average list price, or some other figure when you put your house up for sale?

Tip

When possible, ask at least the average *list price*. If you ask the average listing price, you can expect to get the average sales price.

In reality, however, average list and sales prices are only indicators, clues, hints. The best price you can get may be something quite different.

Trap

Don't make the mistake of listing your home for the *average sales price*. Except in a hot market, buyers don't come in at list price, they tend to offer less. If you ask the average sales price, you'll probably end up selling for a lower figure. To get the average sales price, you normally have to ask the average list price.

Adding Buyer's Perspective and Market Comparables Together

At the beginning of this chapter you were asked to look at your home realistically, to see it as a buyer might see it. For many readers I'm sure that was an education in itself. But even after seeing the house realistically, drawing conclusions regarding price may have been difficult because you didn't really know the market.

Now, after visiting an agent and getting sales and list prices, you should have a much better idea of the market. You should know what comparables are selling for in your area.

Trap

Don't get sidetracked when friends or agents suggest using other approaches to evaluating your house. There are a variety of other methods (besides looking at comparables) for analyzing the value of property such as the "cost approach," where value is determined by cost of rebuilding, or the "income approach," where value is determined by the potential rental income of the house. There are other methods as well.

Forget all these methods. They are great for income producing investment property. But for residential real estate, there is only one realistic approach and that is to check comparables as you've done. The comparable method is not only the approach preferred by competent appraisers, it is the one that lenders rely upon almost entirely. Lenders, after all, may have more to lose than you in a sale since they lend 80 percent of the sales price or more to buyers.

Making the Price Decision

Now, make a best guess decision on the value of your house. Consider the market and comparables, then add or subtract according to the value of your particular home. If you've read the last chapter, you should have a pretty good idea by now of how to size up the value of your particular residence in terms of buyer's perspective. You should now also have a pretty good idea of what comparables are selling for. Use the worksheet on page 24 to help you make your pricing decision.

But Can You Afford to Sell for That Price?

I can remember once going into a home that was owned by an elderly gentleman who had emphysema. He made it quite plain that the only real investment he had in the world was his house and that he wanted to sell it to me. He carefully explained that he had the following mortgages on the house:

First	$55,000
Second	15,000
Third	5,000
Fourth	6,000
Total	$81,000

PRICING DECISION WORKSHEET

Average price of comparable $_____

	Add	Subtract	
1. Better/Worse neighborhood	$_____	$_____	
2. Age of your home (over seven years, subtract, under seven add)	$_____	$_____	
3. Condition of your home (take it all into account—you may want to make a sublist of pluses and minuses)	$_____	$_____	
Totals	$_____	$_____	

Add or subtract to average price of comparable $_____

Adjusted price of your home $_____

Average softness of the market (a percentage you found earlier between list and sales prices)

Now use the average percentage to increase your sales price to a realistic asking price × %_____

List price for your house $_____

He explained that he had so much indebtedness on the property because of his illness. He had borrowed to pay hospital bills. The third and fourth mortgages were actually liens put on his property by a doctor and a nursing home.

He then went on to explain that he needed to get $50,000 cash out of his house. He needed that to pay for his continuing medical treatment. If I could find someone to give him that money, he would sign in a minute.

I had already checked comparables, the neighborhood, and the condition of his house. In my opinion, it wasn't worth more than $85,000, tops. He really didn't even have enough equity to pay his normal closing costs, let alone give him $50,000 in cash out. I didn't see how he could get any cash at all out.

As carefully as I could, I tried to explain the *realities* of the situation to him. He listened patiently until I was finished and then said, "That's all well and good, but I still need to get $50,000 out of the sale!"

The point here is that what you can afford (or want) to sell your home for is irrelevant when it comes time to sell. The sales price is determined by what a buyer who is ready, willing, and able will pay for the property. The fact that you have it mortgaged for more than that amount or that you want a specific cash out for more than the realistic sales price just doesn't matter.

It's a shame, it's sometimes sad, but these are the facts. As Jesse Livermore (who made $22 million in stocks during the depression, then lost $20 million of it in commodities) once said, "There ain't no money lying on the streets and if there was, ain't nobody shoveling it into your pocket." The market ultimately determines the highest sales price of your house, not you.

Now, Consult a Broker or an Appraiser

You've done your homework and you have an excellent idea of what your house is worth. But, you're still not sure. You would like the stamp of approval of a professional. It's time to call in an appraiser.

You can get an appraiser to give you a qualified *opinion* as to the value of your house. The cost is usually under $500, often much less. Look for an appraiser in the phone book under that heading. Find an appraiser who has either an MAI or SREA designation.

A registered appraiser will probably give you a lengthy written opinion of value. It will undoubtedly take into account comparables as well as, perhaps, the cost and the income approach. Of course, the bottom line is that it will give you, presumably, one figure—the value of your home. See how it compares with the figure you arrived at by checking comparables.

You can also get a broker to give you an opinion as to the value of your home. Most brokers will do this for free, in the hopes of getting a listing out of you. Of course you need not list just to get an appraisal.

Trap

If you want to have a broker appraise your property, make sure that the broker gives you a *written* appraisal and that it is understood up front that there will be no charge. Recently some agents have been offering appraisals, then sending the owner a bill for several hundred dollars for the "work." These agents are not in the business of selling real estate, but in the business of making appraisals. Beware of them. Be sure you have it in writing that either the appraisal is free or that, if there is a charge, you know up front what it is and that you agree to it. Quite frankly, I would not normally pay for any appraisal given by a real estate agent or anyone else who was not a professional appraiser.

Most brokers who are willing to give you an appraisal just use the comparable approach described above. Typically, even before they come out to meet you they've looked up your neighborhood and comparables for your size home. Once at your house, they just check its condition and mentally knock off a few dollars or add a few on.

The Best Appraiser

All of which is to say that the appraisal you carefully and *honestly* make for yourself of your own home is probably just as valid as that made by any broker or registered appraiser. I might not trust you to appraise an office building or a commercial lot, but I do trust you to appraise your own home.

Besides, your own appraisal has one big advantage. You can totally trust yourself. You know the work you did and the effort you put forth.

Yes, it's nice to see if an appraiser and, more likely, an agent roughly agree with you. If they don't, you may want to check to see that you—or they—didn't make some gross error. But it's feeling that certainty that you've got the right price, it's not worrying that someone is pulling the wool over your eyes, that's really nice.

And just remember, later on when an agent or buyer tries to knock the price down, you'll have the confidence to hold to your price because you'll *know* what your house is really worth.

3

Selling by Owner vs. Getting an Agent

I have a real estate agent friend who thinks she may be going out of business. The reason is that the last two houses she thought she was going to get a listing on, sold by owner. The owners put up a sign, and within a few weeks each found buyers for their properties.

While this may not be very good news for my agent friend, it seems like excellent news for owners. Yes, you can sell a home on your own, if you're careful and know what you're doing.

In the case of my real estate agent friend, each of the owners paid her a set fee, $1000, to handle the paper work for them. She agreed to do it to maintain good public relations, but she also told me that she can't stay in business on $1000 a deal when she's used to getting $5000.

Can You Sell Your Home by Yourself?

The great incentive, of course, is to save the commission. Commissions these days are typically between 5 and 7 percent. This means on a $100,000 sale, you could save between $5000 and $7000. Quite an incentive. But can you do really do it?

To help you find the answer, consider the questions below.

Are you in a hot market?

If you're in a hot market, your chances of selling by owner are dramatically increased. A hot market means that there are more buyers than sellers. It means that there are buyers searching the papers and cruising the streets of your neighborhood trying to find homes for sale. In this kind of a market your chance of coming up with a buyer are pretty darn good. (See the first two chapters if you're not sure what constitutes a hot market.)

Have you ever sold a home of your own before?

If you haven't, then I would discourage you from trying to sell on your own the first time out. Just like doing your own taxes, it's better if you have an expert do it the first time. That way you can see how a deal is handled and get a feel for the steps involved. That doesn't mean that you can't do it the first time you try. It just means that the chances of your getting yourself in trouble or ruining what otherwise would be a good deal are too great to warrant doing it.

Are you aware of the legal requirements for selling a home in today's market?

In the old days you just found a buyer, took a deposit, opened escrow, and that was about it, except for the signing of documents and the receipt of your check. Today however, things are different. Buyers have become finicky and are much more ready to demand rescission of a sale or cancellation of a deal, and if you haven't protected yourself in terms of warranties, disclosures, and the like, you could be in trouble.

Of course, that doesn't mean you can't learn (much of what you need to know is explained in this book) or can't hire someone to handle the ins and outs for you. In the opening example, the sellers hired a real estate agent to handle the tricky parts of the deal for them. That's one good solution.

Are you psychologically prepared to handle lookers and buyers?

You may think this is a minor consideration, but don't be fooled. Yes, we're all people, and buyers are just nice people looking for a home. But the moment they become potential buyers of your home, they also become adversaries. Their goals are exactly the opposite of yours. They are trying to get the price down; you want to keep it up. They want you to throw in the refrigerator, the furniture, maybe even the cat. You want to take everything with you. They want you to finance the house at 3 percent interest. You want them to get their own loan or pay you 20 percent interest.

I think the point is clear. When dealing with buyers, you're going to have to be prepared to tackle an often aggressive adversary. The buyers are going to make you sweat, make you worry, even make you fearful. Are you ready to cope with that?

If not, then don't try selling yourself.

Are you prepared to give up weekends and evenings waiting for buyers to call or come by?

Buyers don't do anything at your convenience. They do everything at their own convenience. They figure that if they're going to spend $100,000, more or less, on a house, then you, the seller, better cater to them. That means that you have to be ready to show the place at the drop of a hat. A couple drives by, sees your home, and stops in. But, you tell them, you haven't dressed, you haven't cleaned the house, and you've got a terrible headache.

Okay, they say, there are other houses to see and plenty of agents who'll show them. Damn, you think, and let them in. Are you prepared for that? If not, you're going to miss a lot of buyers.

Can you handle buyers' questions on financing?

You can reasonably believe that it's the buyers' obligation to get their own financing. However, if you believe that, you're not living in the real world. Most home buyers know far more about their Visa card than about financing a home. They expect the agent, or you in this case, to help them out. If you don't know, and they don't know, frustration can quickly set in, and an otherwise possible deal can go out the window.

These questions and answers are not designed to discourage you from selling your home, but instead they attempt to show you realistically what you are up against. There are ways around most of the problems as we'll see at the end of this chapter. It won't do you any good to try to sell your home by yourself only to discover that you're totally unprepared to handle the sale.

When to Use an Agent

Just as there are reasons to consider selling a home by yourself, there are also reasons to consider using an agent to move your property.

An agent can probably move your house easier than you when the market is warm or cool.

In a cold market, only God can sell a house! As described in an earlier chapter, in a warm or cool market, buyers tend to be finicky. They want to find just the right house with a minimum of stress and effort. Agents offer them this and, consequently, may be your best bet.

Trap

One of the biggest misunderstandings that sellers have is to think that a buyer who sees their ad in the paper is going to come out and buy their house. Buyers almost never buy homes from ads.

Real estate agents put ads in the paper for two reasons: The first is to get buyers to walk in the agent's door. Agents know that buyers almost never buy the home they saw in the newspaper ad. But once in the door, the agent can qualify the buyers, find out what kind of a home they really want and can really afford, and then can direct them to it.

You the seller, on the other hand, only have one home to sell. When buyers call on an ad and then decide your home isn't what they're looking for, you can't direct them elsewhere. Similarly, without an agent, no one is going to direct them to you.

The other reason agents put ads in the paper is to get listings. Sellers are impressed by an agent's advertising and often will list with the agent who has the most or the biggest ads.

An agent can screen buyers.

When you're selling by owner, you pretty much have to admit anyone who comes to your home. You don't know whether they're a prospective buyer, a hoodlum, or a druggie looking to rob until they are inside your house and you have a chance to talk with them. An agent, on the other hand, presumably screens each person before bringing a potential buyer to your home.

A few years ago this wasn't a big consideration. But today, particularly in urban areas, it's a major consideration.

An agent can financially qualify buyers

Remember, most buyers don't really know what they can afford. An agent, if he or she is any good, can qualify buyers and determine up front whether or not they can afford your home. Thus, buyers who come to see your property should only be ones who can afford to buy it. In addition, once a sale is made, the agent can handle the buyer's financing needs.

An agent can act as an intermediary.

To me, this represents the biggest service that an agent can perform. Let's say that you're selling by owner and a potential buyer comes in who's interested in your house. The buyer looks around and then starts complaining about this and that—little things. If you're a sales person, you know that this is a sure sign the buyer is seriously interested.

So, you pop the question. "Do you want to buy?"

The buyer nods and says, "I think so...If we can come to terms."

Come to terms? What's there to decide, you wonder. There's the price. Pay it and the house is yours. But, you realize that the buyer isn't likely to pay what you're asking. So you wait for the buyer to make an offer.

Only the potential buyer looks uneasy. He or she starts fidgeting with clothes, then walks outside for another look. Before you realize what's happened, the buyer has driven off !

What went wrong?

Chances are it isn't that the buyer didn't want to buy. Quite the contrary, this person might have been very excited about the house. The problem is you.

You showed the buyer around. You probably pointed out your favorite room, the daisies you planted last spring, where your son fell out of the tree and broke his leg, and so on. The buyer saw how personal your house was to you.

On the other hand, the buyer wasn't stupid, and had no intention of paying full price. A typical buyer wants a bargain.

But, how could the buyer reconcile this understanding of how much the place meant to you with the desire to get a rock-bottom low price? Ultimately, the buyer was afraid that if he or she offered you a low price you'd be insulted. Who knows, you might even have yelled and carried on. So the buyer took the easiest way out—and left.

On the other hand, if an agent were involved, the buyer could have separately consulted with the agent. The buyer could have explained concerns and the desire to get a lower price. Finally, the buyer would have felt confident making a lower offer through the agent. That way the buyer wouldn't have to face you. The buyer could even have gotten mad at you and taken it out on the agent.

On the other hand, when the agent (not the buyer) came in with a lower offer, you could have taken your frustration and anger out on the agent *and not imperiled a potential deal.* Upon hearing a low offer you might say things that a buyer might find offensive, but not an agent. You can say almost anything to an agent and still move forward.

The point is that the agent makes the perfect intermediary. You can feel comfortable ranting and raving at the buyers, and they can feel comfortable doing the same to you, all the while never getting personal, never insulting, never straining or ruining the potential deal. The agent makes all of this possible and, in so doing, makes many deals that otherwise couldn't be made.

An agent can handle all the paperwork.

This includes opening escrow, dealing with the necessary disclaimers and warranties that you may have to make, and seeing to it that your sale complies with the real estate law requirements in your area.

In other words, an agent offers you a great deal. Of course, an agent also charges a great deal. Ultimately you have to decide if what the agent charges is worth the cost to you.

To help you in this decision, for the remainder of this chapter, we're going to examine some of the techniques and tricks you can use to sell your home by yourself. At the end of this chapter, you should have enough knowledge to make an intelligent decision on whether or not to try selling your home on your own.

Techniques to Help You Sell Your Own Home

Advertising and Signs

When you sell your own home you become a FSBO (For Sale By Owner). This is what agents call you, and it's how many savvy buyers refer to you. For some buyers the term has particular appeal. They hope that by dealing directly with you, you'll cut the price down further than you would if an agent were involved. The idea is that you won't be paying a commission so you'll split some of that cost with them. Maybe you will and maybe you won't. Regardless, your first task is to let prospective buyers know that you are a FSBO. The local newspaper is an excellent way to do this.

When sellers advertise their own homes, they often make the classic mistake of saying too much in the ad (and of paying too much for it as well). I've seen sellers take out full column, even double column ads for their home, unnecessarily spending hundreds of dollars. Perhaps they are hoping to compete with agents' ads.

Of course, agents are trying to lure in buyers and sellers for many different properties as well as to get listings, you only have one home and aren't interested in listings. Hence, you shouldn't, really can't compete with them. Further, there are only a few essentials that you need to put into an ad. Four or five lines in the classifieds should do it. If that doesn't bring in buyers, be sure your price is realistic and that the market isn't too cool for you to effectively sell your own home. Here are the essential items to include in an FSBO ad:

1. Indicate you're selling by owner (a big come-on).

2. Give the number of bedrooms and baths in the house.

3. Give the style of the home and the neighborhood location (but not the address)—include any special features.

4. Give the price.

5. Give the general condition of the property.

6. Give your phone number or a number where you can be reached.

Here's a typical ad from a newspaper:

For Sale By Owner

Lovely 4 bed, 3 bath home with large pool and fireplace. Located in exclusive Maple School district. Just repainted inside and out, landscaped, owner anxious $105,000 555-2134.

A certain amount of the ad, admittedly, is puffery. "Lovely" is definitely a matter of perspective. "Anxious" means that you want to sell (else why would you be advertising), but suggests that the buyer might be able to work with the price. Other than this, the ad contains the six items necessary.

Would a bigger ad be better? Most advertising specialists say bigger is better because it's easier to see. However, in the case of homes for sale by owners, buyers are probably checking each ad in the classified, so the cost of a big ad might just be wasted. In addition, a bigger ad might just show how inexperienced you really are at selling a home. Finally, anything else you might add at this point might scare away as many buyers as it attracts. For example, you list that the home has a dog runway. There might be more buyers who don't have dogs and don't want runways than do.

If you still feel uncomfortable in designing an ad, run down to your local library or bookstore. There are at least a dozen good books on designing advertising that gets results. Check one out and follow its advice.

A sign is usually a must. It doesn't have to be elaborate. You can usually find ready made FSBO signs at stationery stores for just a few dollars. Plant the sign firmly in the lawn where it can most easily be seen by passersby.

Be sure to put your phone number on the sign. Some sellers also add, "By Appointment Only." That doesn't mean that a potential buyer won't come rapping at your door, but it tends to suggest to most that a call first might be in order.

Trap

Some locales have sign ordinances. These may restrict the number of signs you can use, their size, or even whether or not you're allowed to put a sign out at all. Check with your local building department if you have any questions here.

Showing the Property

There are several concerns here, the biggest of which is that you're letting people into your house without really knowing who they are or what their ulterior motives might be. For some sellers this is no problem. For others, it's a big concern. If it concerns you, get an agent. There's really no other good solution.

When you do show the property, warmly welcome the prospective buyers and point out a few of the amenities of the house. After you've talked for a few moments, allow the buyers to wander through the property themselves. They need to be able to feel that it's their own house.

Trap

Put away any valuables in your rooms. You never know who's honest and who's a thief. Buyers wandering through might just slip a necklace or watch into their pocket and be gone.

Tip

Take a photo of your house (one view of the front, another inside) and make a list of all its features. Get this printed up at a local copy shop including a map showing exactly where your house is located. Be sure your name and phone number is included. Give everyone who comes in a copy. A buyer may want to come back later and not be able to find the property or may want to call you and not have your phone number. This is an excellent method of recalling both.

Also, have a guest book located conveniently near the front door. Ask all potential buyers to sign their names and give their phone numbers. This gives you a record of who came through. Later you can call the buyers or if you subsequently list with an agent, the agent can call them.

Dealing With the Documents

There are a large number of documents that are involved in the sale of your house. These include:

The sales agreement (deposit receipt)

Disclosure forms

Escrow instructions

Termite and other clearances

Deeds

And yet more. If you're like most people, these documents will seem arcane and forbidding to you. Do you have the right ones? Are they filled out properly? Is something or some document missing?

Trap

Don't try to fill out any of the sales documents unless you're a competent attorney. Selling a house involves legally binding actions. If you fill out a document incorrectly and later on trouble results, you can't simply say that you didn't know. You should have known.

Get a competent professional to fill out all documents for you. There are several possibilities.

1. Hire a real estate agent for a set fee to do this task. As noted at the beginning, some agents are willing to do this. (Today, fewer agents will take on the job because of the potential liability.)

2. Hire a real estate attorney. Chances are you're going to need one sooner or later in the transaction. Hire an attorney right at the beginning to draft all documents.

Trap

If you hire an attorney, be sure the attorney is a *real estate* specialist. Most attorneys aren't, and they can muck up a deal by knowing enough generally, but not enough specifically about the transaction.

3. Get an escrow officer to handle some of the documents for you. Be aware, however, that escrow officers are not real estate agents or law-

yers. Their knowledge could be limited in critical areas. You might want to have an agent or attorney handle the deposit receipt and disclosures and the escrow officer the remaining paper work.

Arranging the Financing

Ninety-nine percent of buyers do not pay cash. They expect to get a mortgage or trust deed for 80 percent or more of the purchase price. Thus, one of the biggest problems that you face when selling your own property is helping the buyer arrange the financing. On the surface this can seem an insurmountable problem. Once tackled directly, however, it's not really all that difficult—providing you're not going to try any fancy or creative financing.

Essentially you need to be able to tell the buyers that you have talked to some lenders and that you have determined that a new first mortgage on your property is obtainable, if they will simply contact certain lenders. This doesn't leave the buyers out in the cold and on their own.

What you need to do is to contact a couple of savings and loans or mortgage bankers. Talk to the lending officers and find out their procedures for handling financing. Get their charges and fees and prepare a short "shopping list." Update this at least weekly. Your list should include:

Name of lender

Maximum loan amounts

Points charged (each point equals 1 percent of the loan)

Other fees for the loan

Now, when buyers seem interested, you can hand them the list and suggest they contact one of the lenders. If the buyers are "first-timers," you may even want to go with them to the lender to smooth out any rough spots, although most buyers prefer to keep their personal finances private.

Setting Up Escrow

What could be simpler. After a buyer has signed a sales agreement to purchase your home, just take the document down to a local escrow company. The escrow company will take it from there.

Trap

Don't expect advice, or at least good advice, from the escrow officer. Escrow companies are neutral third parties. In most cases they know their job fairly well. They'll prepare all the necessary documents to close the deal, and they'll tell you what actions, documents, or monies have to be deposited to escrow in order to make the deal.

But, don't expect your escrow officer to answer questions such as, "Which termite inspection company should I use?" or, "The buyer wants me to repaint the interior, but I don't want to—how do we resolve this?"

Those are problems you'll have to resolve with the buyer.

Tip

Very often the various people involved in the sale will provide the necessary information and direction to help close the sale. The loan officers, for example, will often help the buyer straighten out credit problems. The real estate attorney will help you clear up title problems. The escrow officer will provide the document for a second mortgage, if you need it. And so forth.

In most cases, once you have found buyers who have signed a purchase agreement, the remainder of the transaction will progress smoothly. In most cases you should have few to no problems, assuming you know the basics of a sale.

However, in some cases problems arise. These can take many forms:

Disputes with the buyer

Serious title problems

Buyer's inability or lack of desire to perform

A sudden increase in interest rates keeping the buyer from qualifying

A physical problem with your house

Problems with local government bodies such as the building department or planning commission

It's at this point that you may very well need expert help. Your real estate attorney can provide some of it, particularly in matters of legality. But in matters of common sense and in disputes, your best ally is a real estate agent. You may need to bring an agent in either for a fixed fee or for a percentage of the sale. Of course, if you already have a buyer, you wouldn't expect to pay the agent a full commission.

Making the Big "FSBO" Decision

These, then, are your many potential problems as well as your options. Should you hire an agent? Or should you try to sell by yourself?

Try this decision checklist to help you make up your mind.

FSBO Decision Checklist

		YES	NO
1. What's the condition of housing market in your area?	Hot [ ] Warm [ ] Cool [ ] Cold [ ]		
2. Do you understand the steps to selling a home?		[ ]	[ ]
3. Are you up-to-date on the disclosure requirements, needed documents, and real estate law in your area?		[ ]	[ ]
4. Are you ready to handle a throng of people looking through your home?		[ ]	[ ]
5. Are you comfortable with letting strangers enter your house?		[ ]	[ ]
6. Will you give up your weekends and evenings in the hope that a buyer will call or come by?		[ ]	[ ]
7. Do you have a plan for handling the sales agreement? Who will fill it out?		[ ]	[ ]
8. Do you have a plan for handling disputes with the buyer both before an offer is presented and afterward?		[ ]	[ ]
9. Have you worked out the financing so that you can give the buyer options?		[ ]	[ ]
10. Have you contacted an escrow company, a real estate attorney, an agent, and have each agreed to handle their specific parts of the deal?		[ ]	[ ]
11. Have you readied an ad, and are you willing to stick a "For Sale By Owner" sign in your front yard?		[ ]	[ ]

The hotter the market and the more "Yes" answers you give, the more likely it is that you'll be able to successfully sell your property on your own.

Before you ultimately decide, however, here's one last bit of advice. Remember that regardless of how high a real estate agent's fee may be, the agent performs a service and earns that money.

But, you may say, the agent is charging a 6 percent commission on a $150,000 house, or $9000. What is the agent doing for that money?

The answer is that the agent has spent the time to learn the real estate law in your area. The agent has set up a place of business and advertises in order to attract clients who may become your potential buyers. The agent is prepared to handle the transaction from beginning to end, including the sales agreement, the documents, the escrow, helping to arranging financing, and handling the closing. In addition, the agent, in most areas, is paying hefty errors and omissions and malpractice insurance fees that cover you in case the agent does something wrong.

If this sounds like a plea to use an agent, it really isn't. I'm simply pointing out that when you use an agent, a good agent, you do get something for your money.

That doesn't mean you can't do it yourself. In most cases you can. However, your time and your stress are worth something too. Only a fool works for free.

Ultimately your decision has to be whether or not it's worth it to you to work, to learn, to get the stress in selling your own home, for the fee you would otherwise pay an agent. From that perspective, I know of many sellers who feel that the agents' fees are really worthwhile. They feel it's cheaper in the long run.

Tip

One compromise that many sellers use is to set a time limit for selling by themselves. They will try being a FSBO, for example, for one month. If, during that time, they haven't sold the property, they will then list with an agent.

This is an excellent plan. It allows you to try to sell it yourself, and it assures you that later on you won't feel that you could have done it, if only you'd tried.

I would only caution that you set a realistic time limit. Perhaps you want to give yourself two months, or even three. The time period doesn't matter, as long as you aren't in a rush to sell.

If you sell, great. But determine that you'll use an agent if you still haven't sold the house by a certain time. Otherwise, you could be spending a very long and frustrating time without any accomplishment to show for it.

4
Hiring the Right Broker

There's an old adage in the real estate business that goes, "Those who list, last." It means that the key to success *for an agent* is to get as many listings as possible. As some of those listings sell, the agent is provided with a continual stream of income. Thus many agents have become quite adept at gathering listings. However, what's good for the agent may not necessarily be good for you.

Tip

The words "broker," "agent," "associate," and "salesperson" are all part of the same family. They all mean a person licensed by the state to sell real estate. A *broker* can operate an office and work independently. An *associate* or a *salesperson* (the two terms are synonymous) means that while the person has a license, it is not a full license. An associate or a salesperson must work for a broker, under that broker's license. It doesn't mean they aren't good at selling. It usually means that either they haven't had enough experience yet to get a broker's license (most states require several years) or they are more comfortable working for someone else than for themselves. An *agent* means either a broker or salesperson or associate. Agent is the generic term for any licensed real estate person. (Realtor is a registered trademark of the National Association of Realtors, a trade organization. Only brokers-members can use it.)

The last thing you want to do is to list your property with an agent who "gathers" listings. Chances are that once you sign the listing agreement that's the last you'll see of your agent. If some other agent sells the house, great. But don't count on that lister of yours to push your property.

You Want an Active Agent

The key, of course, is to list with someone who takes a strong, active interest in your property. I have a friend, Sarah, who is what I consider to be the best real estate agent a seller could ever find.

Sarah is a broker who owns and operates her own office. She only has about three (the number varies) salespeople working for her at any given time, so she doesn't have to be constantly supervising them. Instead, she handles property directly on her own. Sarah is what I call a "full service" agent. She lists property and she also sells it.

Sarah has been in business for about 15 years and she knows her community like the post office does. If you give her the address of your home (assuming it's in her community), frequently she can tell you off the top of her head what nearby houses have sold for in the last year or two. With just a walk through your home, she can give you a sales price that I would bank on. Sarah is that good.

Of course, the real reason that Sarah is so good at what she does is that she loves to sell. For her, real estate isn't work, it's pleasure. She's up by seven every morning—out in the field going to see the properties newly listed by other brokers and placed on the Multiple Listing Service. In the afternoons, evening, and weekends, when buyers usually call from her ads, she quickly hooks their interest with her knowledge, qualifies them, and then takes them to see properties, of course, pushing her own listings first. She also pushes her listings to other brokers, talking the properties up at weekly broker meetings. She gives her listings the widest possible circulation in terms of letting brokers, as well as potential buyers, know they're for sale.

Sarah has an enviable track record. She has sold over 95 percent of all properties she has ever listed. Nearly all of those sales came within two months of the listing date.

Would I list with her? You bet, in a moment, without a second's hesitation.

The question for you is, how do you find an agent like Sarah to list your home?

Locating a Good Agent

For many of us who don't know a "Sarah," the place we usually turn is the yellow pages of the phone book. There are better ways, which we'll see later in this chapter. But for now, let's consider what you see if you look in the yellow pages. Chances are that if you're new to real estate, you'll see names of independent offices which you may not recognize as well as the names of franchise offices which may be very familiar to you. Some of the franchise advertising may be quite big. Many sellers simply save time and go with the known, the franchise name that they've heard before.

Franchise vs. Independent

Twenty years ago virtually all real estate agents were independent. Today, the majority belong to some franchise such as Century 21, ERA, Coldwell Banker, and so on. These are big names and big companies. Thus, one of the first questions that most sellers ask is, should I go with a franchise or with an independent?

The question is irrelevant. One of the best tips this book can give you is that you should go with the best agent you can find. If that agent happens to be associated with a franchise, great. If they're independent, as Sarah was, just as great. Don't make your listing decision based solely on the sign in front of the office. Here's why.

In nearly all states, a real estate office must be operated by a broker licensed in that state. The licensed broker has the choice of hanging out a shingle with the broker's name on it (or some other made-up name) or buying into one of the many national franchises.

Many brokers opt for the franchise. The reason is quite simple. Let's take an example from the fast food business. You drive into a town you've never been in before. You want something to eat. You want the meal to be fast and inexpensive, the premises to be clean and pleasant, and the food to be safe and at least minimally tasty. How are you going to pick?

You could take your chances with the local diner, or you could stop at a few stores and ask people their opinion. Or you drive directly to McDonald's, Burger King, Wendy's, or the like.

The national fast-food chains all maintain standards so that whether you go into one in Seattle or in Orlando, you know you'll get the same quality of service and food. (One of the most surprising visits to a fast-food chain that I ever made was to a jam-packed Burger King on the Champs Élysées in Paris. The food was extraordinaire!)

A real estate franchisee affords the same name recognition and resulting business. Most real estate franchisers offer their franchisees advertising, office management help, forms, even colorful jackets, in addition to their signs and "colors." I know many real estate brokers who have doubled their income overnight by converting from being independent to being a franchise.

That's what a franchise offers brokers and why so many participate. The real question, of course, is what does a franchise offer *you?*

Franchise Pluses

As just discussed, they offer at least a minimal standard of performance. One office tends to look like another, and in general the agents tend to be fairly well trained. In addition they also offer long-distance moving assistance. List your home with a franchise in one city, and an agent from a linked franchise in another city can already be looking for a new home for you.

In my opinion the true value of the franchise is that they bring a degree of order, of homogeneity to real estate.

Independent Pluses

On the other hand there are the independents. They have limited advertising and name recognition. To make up for this they usually have to work harder.

Tip

Just because an office is independent many people conclude that the agents have to be better in order to make it on their own. This doesn't necessarily have to be true. The agents could just as easily be so terrible that no franchise would take them.

On the other hand, a very good salesperson (or group of them) could be working independently (such as Sarah was) and simply not want to give a percentage of each deal to the franchise company.

What's important to understand, however, is that where it counts, in selling, the independents can usually offer just as much as the franchises. The reason is the listing services.

It's important to understand that both the independents and the franchise offices belong to the same listing services (typically the MLS—Multiple Listing Service) in their area, and since nearly all houses are listed on the services, all agents whether independent or franchised usually work on the same properties.

Thus an independent often has just as big a base of listings to work from as a franchise.

Questions on Franchises vs. Independents

This, then, is basically the condition of the marketplace with regard to franchises and independents. However, you may still have some questions such as those listed below:

Question: Won't the franchise offer better service?

Answer: The franchise can offer name recognition, trained personnel, and, usually, more advertising. That doesn't necessarily translate into better service for you. Selling real estate remains a highly individualized operation. Remember, it's how much your lister pushes your property that counts.

Question: Won't the franchise back up the actions of its sales people?

Answer: Good question. Be sure to ask the franchisee. Some do, at least minimally. Some don't. It depends on what the problem is.

Question: What happens if I go to an independent and he or she makes a big mistake that costs me money?

Answer: Today nearly all real estate agents carry errors and omissions as well as some form of malpractice insurance. In addition some states, such as California, maintain funds to at least partially compensate people who have been victimized by bad agents. Ask your independent what protections are offered.

My Choice

My own preference, as noted at the beginning of this section, is to pay little to no attention to the sign in front of the office. Instead, I judge the person I'm dealing with.

It's important to understand that this discussion is not intended to knock or praise either franchises or independents. I repeat, my advice is to go with the best agent you can find.

Finding a Good Agent

A good first step is to ask your friends if they know someone who has recently sold a home. There are so many agents around, close to 1 percent of the population in some areas, that almost everyone knows one. Did they have a good experience? Talk to the person. Ask them if they would recommend the agent. Ask them if they have any reservations about the agent.

Trap

Know your friends. Some agents pay a "finder's fee" to former clients who will recommend them to sellers. A good friend is more interested in your well-being than a few bucks for a finder's fee. Just be sure you're dealing with a good friend.

Interviewing Agents

If you can't get a recommendation, then it's up to you to find an agent. That's easy. Just put a FSBO (explained in the last chapter) sign in your front lawn. You'll have agents climbing all over you trying to get your listing. Finding a good agent is a bit more difficult.

I don't recommend starting out with a sign in your front lawn. Rather, pick a real estate office that's nearby and check it out. Walk in and tell the receptionist or the salesperson who greets you that you want to talk to the broker. Don't explain why, yet.

When the broker appears, explain that you are *thinking* of listing your house. You want to list with an office that's *active*. In fact, you'd like to list with the best salesperson (not lister) in the office. But for now, you want to learn something about the office itself.

For example, how many listings does the office currently have? If the office is active, the broker will be delighted to point out the many listings. If the office is a dud, there won't be many or any. Leave.

Trap

Be sure to ask for listings taken by agents in this office. Don't be fooled if the broker simply takes out a book and shows you all the listings on the MLS. None of them may belong to that office.

Now ask how many of its own listings *this office* has sold in the past six months. The broker should know exactly. If they haven't sold any or there's any hemming and hawing, leave.

Along the way, listen carefully to what the broker says. Is there one name of one agent that keeps popping up? Is that agent, in fact, the best seller in the office?

At the end of your brief discussion, ask the broker who would be the best seller in the office in terms of sales (not listings) made. Most brokers will chuckle at your audacity, but will also probably give you a straight answer. Is it the same name that kept popping up in your earlier conversation?

Now go see that person. Introduce yourself, and ask not only how many properties this person has sold, but how many were listed in the past six months? You want to deal with a good salesperson, but also one who handles listings, not just the sales end of the business.

Ask if you can have a list with phone numbers of the sellers of listings that this agent recently sold. Explain that you'd like to call them to see what they thought of the service.

This is the acid test. Most sellers never ask to see such a list. They wouldn't think of it. After all, it sounds like you're asking to see something confidential.

Tip

It's not confidential. Sales of homes are all recorded and are all public knowledge. If you want to take the time to go down to the court house, you can compile your own list of recent sellers.

A strong agent, one who will work for you, will be *delighted* to give you a list of recent sellers. After all, what does the agent do but please clients? A weak agent will give you reasons why the list cannot be given out. Leave.

Tip

In some offices, particularly the larger ones, the top agents' names are often posted on the signs on the walls and, in some cases, even their pictures. Just look carefully as you enter and your questions may be answered.

Other Areas of Concern

While knowing that the agent is a great salesperson is an enormous plus for you, you also need to know something more about this person. You want to be sure the person is competent in the real estate business, is honest in dealings, and is reliable.

You may want to ask the following questions to help you determine these things:

1. *How long have you been in the real estate business?*

The learning curve for real estate is fairly long. The reason is that the numbers of transactions a person can become involved with at any one time is limited. Usually it takes three to five years for an agent to have gotten a well-rounded education. Five to ten years is better.

2. *What professional organizations do you belong to?*

The minimum here should be the local real estate board and multiple listing service as well as the state and National Association of Realtors (NAR). The agent may also be a member of the Chamber of Commerce and local citizens committees, all pluses.

3. *What will you do to expedite the sale of my home?*

The answer here should be immediate, direct, and comprehensive. The agent should explain a plan of action that should sell your house.
   The plan should include:

Listing for a specified time. (Beware of agents who want to list for more than three months except in a cool or cold market.)

Promotion, including talking up the listing at the local real estate board.

Advertising.

Open houses.

These, then, are some of the questions you can ask of your future agent. Here's a checklist to take with you when you interview an agent:

Checklist for Interviewing Agents

1. Houses listed in last six months.   _____
2. Houses sold in the last six months.   _____

	YES	NO
3. References available?	[ ]	[ ]
4. Agent fully licensed?	[ ]	[ ]
5. Been in the real estate business at least 3–5 years.	[ ]	[ ]
6. Belongs to many professional organizations?	[ ]	[ ]
7. Offers a plan for selling my home?	[ ]	[ ]
8. Does not ask for an overly long listing?	[ ]	[ ]

5
Negotiating the Listing and the Commission

Once you've decided to list your home for sale and have found the right agent, it's time to negotiate the listing and the commission. "Oh," some readers may be saying, "*Negotiate* the listing and commission? Aren't those automatically set in advance?"

Yes and no.

Some agents will accept only one kind of listing and only a set minimum rate of commission. Others will negotiate one or the other or both. Generally speaking most good agents will be amenable to some negotiation.

Tip

There is no "set" rate of commission on the sale of real estate. The commission you agree to pay your agent is between you and the agent. A few decades ago real estate boards in certain areas were accepting only those listings which had a minimum rate of commission. Lawsuits and judicial decisions, however, have outlawed that practice. Today, the commission is *totally negotiable*.

Trap

Just because the commission is negotiable is not necessarily a good reason to insist on a low commission rate. You generally get what you pay for. If you offer a commission lower than your next door neighbor who has the same house at roughly the same price, which house do you think agents will be more likely to show?

Reasons to Pay the Agent's Rate

Most rates of commission today for single family residential property are between a low of 3 percent and a high of 7 percent. Let's say your agent walks in and says that she wants 7 percent. Should you pay it?

I had this happen to me several years ago when I was selling a house out of my area. The agent pointed out that, yes, the commission was negotiable. However, she was an excellent salesperson and her track record with sales of listings proved it. True, other offices in the area were only asking between 5 and 6 percent, but she was better than they were. Was I willing, she asked, to pay a lower rate and wait longer, perhaps forever, to sell my property? Wouldn't it be cheaper to pay a higher rate and get a quicker, sure sale?

I mention this example because this same type of argument may be used on you. Be aware, however, that it's most often the lister (agent who only lists) who uses it.

I asked the agent if she would guarantee me a sale. She said she couldn't do that, but then again no one could. (Note: Some offices will guarantee to buy your home at a predetermined price if you don't sell within a set period of time. There are inherent conflicts of interest here and this is discussed later in this chapter.)

I asked if she could guarantee that she would sell my property faster than any other agent. She said she was sure she could sell it quickly. She couldn't guarantee that, but then again, nothing in this world had a guarantee attached to it.

I then asked her why, if she couldn't guarantee anything, she felt she was entitled to a commission higher than other reputable, good agents were charging?

She explained that it was because she was better than they, in her opinion, and would work harder for me.

I pointed out that all potential listing agents I talked with stressed that they were better than the others, that all said they would work hard for a quick sale, and that as far as I could tell, she wasn't offering anything more for the additional rate. And I showed her to the door.

The point here is that while you don't want to try to "cheat" agents into a low fee that will make them not want to serve you, you also don't want to pay an excessive fee either. My suggestion is that you check with several agents to see what the "going rate" is in your area and pay no more...or less than that.

Tip

A good agent will do two things. He will explain why he charges a certain rate and point out that he really can't afford to work for less. If you insist on less, he may accept the listing provided you understand he will in turn provide less than normal service.

Secondly, the good agent won't browbeat you into paying an excessively high commission. Good agents don't get rich by charging higher commissions. They get rich by making more deals.

Why Commissions Are So High

Even though there may be good reasons for paying an agent the asked for commission, one can't help but wonder why the commissions in general are so high.

For example, back in the 1950s the commissions were generally around 5 percent. Several studies have shown that by the 1980s the average commissions have climbed to the 6 and 7 percent range.

In addition, back in the 1950s the average house only cost around $15,000. Today it's over $100,000. That means that back in 1950 an agent who sold a house for $15,000 at a 5 percent commission collected a total of only $750. Today, an agent who sells a $100,000 house for 6 percent collects a commission of $6000. Today's commission is almost eight times higher. Why?

There are three answers to this question:

1. Part of the answer is simple inflation. Things cost many times more today than they did 40 years ago.

2. Another part of the answer is better and more costly license preparation. Back in 1950 all an agent had to do to sell real estate was pass a short test, rent an office, and put out a sign. Today agents' tests often last several days, there may be college or night school requirements, and there may also be apprenticeship requirements. Even the cost of the license itself has gone up. In California, for example, in 1950 a broker's license cost $25 every four years. Today it's $160.

3. Finally there are additional costs today. In the 1990s, agents must pay for several kinds of malpractice insurance as well as have an attorney on call, something that almost no one did back in 1950.

Thus, if agents ask for a higher commission today than 40 years ago, there is some justification for it.

Besides, the agent may not get the whole commission. While you may deal with only one listing agent, by the time your house is sold, there may be as many as four agents involved. In the vast majority of cases there are at least two agents involved.

Typically the commissions are split between agents. The splits vary with fifty-fifty being typical, although sixty-forty (60 percent going to the selling agency and 40 percent to the listing) is also common.

Let's say you sell your home for $100,000. There happen to be two different brokers involved and two different sales people. You listed with a salesperson, the buyer bought through a salesperson. Here's how a typical split of a 6 percent commission might work out.

Listing salesperson	1.5%	$1500
Listing broker	1.5%	$1500
Selling salesperson	1.5%	$1500
Selling broker	1.5%	$1500
Total commission	6.0%	$6000

Instead of a whopping $6000 paid to one person, four agents each get $1500. If the agent is to make $30,000 a year selling houses, that person has to make 20 deals just like yours. That's a lot of deals for an agent.

It's important to understand that I'm not advocating higher commissions or even trying to justify them. It's simply a matter of pointing out that in many cases the commissions aren't as high as they would appear to be on the surface.

Why Not Use a Discount Broker?

In many areas of the country discount brokers are available. These brokers often charge a fixed rate or a rate that may be half the normal commission rate. If the typical rate is, for example, 6 percent in your area, they may charge only 3 percent. On a $100,000 house that could mean the difference between a $6000 commission and a $3000 commission. It could save you $3000. Why not go with a discounter?

You can, and I suggest you do, if you're trying to sell your home by yourself as described in earlier chapters. A discounter may provide just the limited services that you need. But remember, it works best in a hot market. As the market cools off, the discounted listing becomes less and less appealing, because discounters provide fewer services.

Consider this true experience. I was looking for a rental home to buy in a market that I could only describe as warm. I was working with an agent and he was showing me this house and that. I happened to glance over at his listing book (a book which contains pictures as well as listings of homes for sale) and noticed that he always seemed to skip over one page that contained homes presumably in the price range I was looking for.

After a time I asked him if I could look at that book. He hesitated, then complied. He explained he wasn't supposed to show it to someone who wasn't an agent in his area. I suspected he showed it to anyone who asked.

I immediately turned to that page he had been skipping. In addition to others, it contained two homes that looked ideal for my needs. I asked him why we hadn't looked at them. We could, he explained, only he didn't think they were right for me. When I looked closer at the listing I saw that they were both listed by discounters for a 3 percent commission. The truth is they weren't right for him.

Tip

There are several kinds of agents, as we'll see shortly, but the agent showing buyers property owes a loyalty to those buyers to show them all the houses suitable for them. In theory, the agent should never shy away from a house which might be ideal for the buyers, but which provides a lower commission. That's unethical and may even be illegal. The actual practice, however, is sometimes considerably different from the theory.

Other Limitations With Discount Brokers

In addition to reducing the potential exposure to your property, many discount brokers also reduce the services they offer to you. For example, they may not be willing to negotiate with the buyers for you. That could be up to you. Or they could ask you to pay for advertising which, it usually turns out, only benefits them. Or they may not be willing to work with buyers to secure financing or to move a deal through escrow.

In short, a discounter cannot afford to give you what a full-service broker offers because you aren't paying enough. On the other hand, perhaps you don't need full-service. Perhaps what you need is partial service because you're selling your home on your own.

My advice is to let yourself be guided by your needs. If you want a broker to handle your sale, go to a full-service, full-commission broker.

On the other hand, if you're a FSBO seller, then by all means, try a discounter.

The reasons that discounters may be good for you is that:

1. You pay a lower commission.
2. You don't need a full service broker.

The reasons that discounters may not be your best bet is that even though you save money:

1. Your house may get far lower exposure.
2. There may be less advertising.
3. You may have to pay for advertising.
4. The agent may not handle critical paperwork or may not help the buyers secure financing.
5. The agent may not help you in your negotiations with buyers, resulting, ultimately, in your receiving a lower price.

Types of Listing Agreements

There are a variety of listing agreements which an agent can offer you. No, there isn't just one standard one that they all use. Each type of listing has its own pluses and minuses and should be considered depending on your specific needs. The listing agreement will normally say right on the face the type that it is.

Exclusive Right to Sell

This is the type of listing that almost all agents prefer. It is also the type that many listing services prefer. It means the following:

If the agent or anyone else including you sells the house, you owe the agent a commission.

This includes people to whom you showed the house while the listing was in effect, even though you sell it in a period of time after the listing expires.

In other words, with this type of listing you insure the agent of a commission if the house is sold. The only way the agent cannot get a commission is if there is no sale. Agents feel comfortable putting forth 100 percent effort with such a listing since they feel they are protected.

Exclusive Agency

If the agent sells the house, you owe a commission. If you sell it to someone the agent didn't show it to, you don't.

Now, you may be thinking, there's a listing that's more to my liking. Yes and no. Agents have good reasons for not liking this type of listing. They may bring buyers to your home who tell them they're not interested in purchasing. Later, the buyers come to you and negotiate a sale. You claim no commission is due because you had no knowledge that the agent showed these buyers the home; they dealt directly with you. The agent claims that a commission is due because the agent found the buyer.

In this case the agent is right. But, to get that commission the agent might have to go to arbitration or even to court. Along the way there are certain to be hard feelings and agents are very concerned about their reputations in a community. They don't like it to be known that they're having to put pressure on to collect even a justified commission. Thus most agents simply won't work, or won't work hard, on this type of listing.

This listing is sometimes used when you have a buyer or buyers who you think might be interested in purchasing, but who haven't yet committed. You want to list the property and get it onto the market, but you want to exclude paying a commission for those buyers you've already found.

Open Listing

Sometimes called a "vest pocket listing," in an open listing *you agree to pay a commission to any broker who brings you a buyer or to pay no commission if you find the buyer.* Some sellers think this is a good listing because you can give it to any agent.

Most agents, however, won't devote 10 minutes of time to this kind of listing. If buyers should show up who can't be interested in any other piece of property, then they'll bring them to you in a last chance effort at a commission. The possibility of doing work and not getting paid for it is so great here that agents in general just don't want to bother with this type of listing.

About the only time it's used is in bare land when the chances of selling are very slim, and it could take years to produce a buyer. You might simply let every agent know that the property is for sale and you'll pay a commission, but you're not willing to give any one of them an "exclusive."

Guaranteed Sale Listing

This isn't a separate type of listing, rather it's any of the earlier mentioned listings, but is usually the Exclusive Right to Sell. *The listing simply includes a separate clause which says that if the property isn't sold by the end of the listing term, then the agent agrees to buy it from you for a set price—usually the listing price, less the commission.*

Although widely used at one time, these types of listings are often frowned upon today because of their inherent conflict of interest. The reason is simple: while an honest agent can use this listing to induce you to list, a dishonest agent can use it to gain a larger than expected commission.

A dishonest agent may induce an unwary seller to list at a low price, then take no action to sell the property. When the listing expires, the agent buys the house at the previously guaranteed low price and later resells at a much higher price. This is particularly a problem when the listing calls for the agent to buy the property for less than the listed price—justified by the supposed "fact" that it didn't sell for the listed price, meaning that price was too high.

If your agent suggests this type of listing, insist on the following, which may already be legally required in your state:

1. The agent can only buy the property for the listed price. No less.

2. The agent has to inform you of the price, and you have to agree in writing to that price if the agent resells the property to someone else within one year of your sale to the agent.

3. The agent must buy the property. The agent can't sell it to a third party in escrow, unless you get all of the proceeds less the agreed upon commission.

Net Listing

This is by far the most controversial type of listing. *You agree up front on a fixed price for the property. Everything over that price goes to the agent.* You agree to sell for $100,000. If the agent brings in a buyer for $105,000, the agent gets $5000 as the commission. But if the agent brings in a buyer for $150,000 the agent gets $50,000 for a commission.

The opportunities to take advantage of a buyer should be obvious here. An unscrupulous agent could get a listing for a low price and then sell for a high one, getting an unconscionable commission.

A net listing is sometimes useful for a "hopeless" property. For one reason or another, the property isn't saleable. So the buyer tells the agent, "Be creative. Find a buyer. Here's what I want. Everything else is yours."

In such an arrangement you as the seller should insist, if state law doesn't already require it, that you be informed of the final selling price and that you agree in writing to it.

The easiest way to handle a net listing is to simply avoid it.

Which Listing Is Best?

The type of listing that's best for you depends, of course, on your situation and that of your property. In 95 percent of the cases, the listing that is likely to get you the best results is the Exclusive Right to Sell.

In it you give up your right to sell the property. But in exchange you get the best chance of having the agent put forth the best effort in completing the sale.

In addition, you want to be sure that your agent puts your house on a listing service, such as the Multiple Listing Service or whatever cooperative system is in use in your area. That guarantees that your house will get the widest possible exposure.

Tip

In the trade, allowing other agents to work on a listing is called "cobroking" it. Be sure your agent agrees to co-broke your property with all other agents.

Trap

An old line that some agents use is to tell you this, "To give you a better chance at a quick sale, I'll hold back the listing from the cooperative listing service for a few weeks. That'll mean that all the agents in my office will work harder on it. It's really a better opportunity for you."

Don't believe it. It's just a ploy to give the listing agent a chance to sell your property without having to split the commission. During those few weeks before your house gets on the cooperative system, your agent may indeed be working very hard trying to sell it. But that's one agent. On the service, as many as a thousand or more agents will be aware that your house is for sale. One of them may already have a buyer looking for just what you've got.

Don't let the agent "hold back " your listing. Insist that it be given the widest possible exposure at the earliest possible time.

The Listing Agreement

The listing agreement is often several pages long and may contain a considerable amount of legalese. However, there are a number of points that it should contain and that you should watch out for:

1. *Price*: The listing agreement should specify the price you expect to receive for your property.

2. *Deposit*: The agreement should indicate how large a deposit you expect from a buyer. It should also indicate that the agent may take the deposit, but that it is *your money*. Usually such agreements specify that if the buyer doesn't go through with the deal, you and the agent split the deposit.

3. *Terms*: It's important that the terms you are willing to accept are spelled out. For example, if you want only cash, your listing agreement should say that. If you are willing to accept a second mortgage as part of the purchase price, it should specify that as well. In actual practice this doesn't preclude an agent from bringing you a buyer who offers other terms. It just means you don't have to accept such a buyer.

Tip

It's important to be as specific as possible in the sales agreement because once in a great while sellers may choose not to sell even though the agent has produced a buyer who is ready, willing, and able to purchase. In such a case you could be liable for the commission even though you don't sell *unless* the buyer doesn't meet the exact terms of the listing. Spelling out the terms can be very important.

4. *Title Insurance*: Today almost all property sold has title insurance. The only questions are which title company to use and who is going to pay for it. The listing agreement usually specifies both. In most areas title insurance costs are split between buyer and seller, although in some states the seller pays it. Find out what is commonly done in your area...just be sure you don't pay for it if you don't need too.

5. *Keybox*: Buyers come when they're ready, not when you're ready. Therefore, it's a good idea to allow the agent to show the property even when you're not home. Since there may be many cooperative agents, the common way of handling this is to have a keybox installed. The listing agreement asks you to give permission for this.

Trap

Agents and buyers represent a broad spectrum of people. Just as in the general population there are those who are scrupulously honest as well as those who are dishonest, the same holds true in real estate. While thefts from homes with lockboxes installed do occur, it's fairly rare. Therefore, while you have a lockbox on your home, you are well advised to remove all valuables.

Note: In many listing agreements the agents specifically disclaim responsibility for loss due to having a lockbox improperly used.

6. *Sign*: You should give permission for the agent to install a reasonable sign in your front yard. It's an excellent method of attracting buyers, perhaps the best.

7. *Arbitration and attorney's fees*: Typically these agreements call for arbitration in case of a dispute and state that in the case of a lawsuit the prevailing party will have his or her attorney's costs paid by the losing party. This is standard boilerplate.

8. *Disclosure*: The listing agreement should also list the various disclosures that you as a seller must make to a buyer in your state. (These are handled in a separate chapter.)

9. *Equal housing disclosure*: This simply states that you are in compliance with federal and state anti-discrimination laws when you list your property.

10. *Beginning and Expiration Date*: This is perhaps the most critical part of the document. It states when the listing you are giving expires. It should be a written-out date—June 1, 1990, not "in three months." If the date isn't inserted, the agent could insist that the listing you intended to be for three months is actually for much longer.

Tip

I suggest never giving a listing for more than three months. In most markets that should be enough time for a good agent to find a buyer. If there are extenuating circumstances at the end of the three month period, you might want to extend the listing for an additional three months. Or, you might want to secure the services of a different agent.

Trap

Beware of the agent who insists on a long listing. This could be a "lister," an agent who simply takes listings and lets them sit. Giving a longer listing might mean it will take longer to sell your house. My feeling is that no really good agent will normally want more than three months to sell a house. After that if it doesn't sell, it could be overpriced or there could be some problem with it that will keep it from selling indefinitely, and it might not be worth the agent's time to bother with it. Wanting a long term listing is a danger signal.

11. *Commission*: The agreement will state the percentage of commission that you've agreed upon. Beware of a clause right next to it which may state something to the effect that if you take your house off the market for any reason, you owe the agent a fee that is then written in. This is a "liquidated damages" clause and it means that although you may not have to pay the full commission if you decide not to sell, you are committing yourself to paying something, often a substantial amount of money.

In addition to the listing agreement itself, most agents will also provide you with an agent's disclosure document. It is discussed in the next chapter.

Danger Signals

Avoid agents who:

1. Want long-term listings.
2. Insist on very high commissions.
3. Apply pressure to get you to sign. If they pressure you to sign the listing, think what they'll do when a bad offer comes in.
4. Accept any sales price on the listing, even though you know it's too high. They just want you to sign and hope that after a month or so when you can't sell, you'll drop your price.
5. Hedge on the disclosures, saying that you can trust them to look out for your interests.
6. Insist on a listing (net or guaranteed sale) that allows them to make a higher commission, without letting you know that they need your written permission.
7. Want your power of attorney to sign a deal. If you give up your power of attorney the agent could accept an offer for you that you really don't want.

6

The Agent's Duties and Responsibilities to You

Listing your home for sale is not a one way street. You agree to pay a hefty commission to the agent. But that agent also agrees to give you something in return. That something includes:

Service

Loyalty

Diligence

Honesty

Disclosure of facts

Skill

Care

Some of the above may actually be stated in the listing agreement. Others are considered part of the agent's fiduciary responsibilities. All are considered examples of ethical conduct.

However, unless you are fully aware of the exact nature of your agent's duties and responsibilities to you, you may not realize that your agent isn't performing up to snuff. In this chapter we'll go over what the agent owes you. (Note: Unfortunately this is the chapter that readers usually come to when there's a problem with their listing agent. If that's your case, be aware that means of getting out of a bad listing agreement are discussed at the end of this chapter.)

Different Agents, Different Duties

When you list with an agent, he owes you loyalty. That takes many forms, but the clearest expression of loyalty is when that agent gets a sales agreement from buyers, and although the buyers are offering, for example, $90,000, the agent tells you that he has overheard them say that they would be willing to pay $95,000 for the house.

That little bit of information is worth $5000. Without it you might have accepted the $90,000 offer. With it you hold out for $95,000...and get it.

Why should the agent be loyal to you and not to the buyer? Why should the agent tell you this little tidbit of information that was worth so much money?

The reason has to do with the agent's fiduciary (position of trust) relationship with you. It is incumbent upon the agent to tell you any fact that may help you in making your decision to sell.

On the other hand, if you tell the agent that you would be willing to accept $85,000 when you're asking $90,000, the agent is not obliged to tell that to the buyers. In fact, because of the fiduciary relationship, the agent is prohibited (in theory) from telling the buyers anything about price or terms that you do not specifically tell the agent to divulge.

In other words, the agent is bound to you in ways that are definitely to your advantage. However, it's important not to get too smug about agents' relationships. Not all agents stick to the letter of ethical conduct, while other agents may have different duties and responsibilities.

Subagents

When you list your property with an agent, she owes you a fiduciary responsibility as described above. But, what if the agent puts your property on the listing service and suddenly a hundred or a thousand agents are all working it. Do they owe you a fiduciary responsibility?

Yes...and no.

If they act as a "subagent," meaning that your agent delegates agency powers to them, then they owe you the same duties and responsibilities. They owe it to you to tell you when the buyers are willing to pay more and not to tell the buyers when you are willing to take less.

However, some agents act independently, although they may still show your house and sell it from the listing service. These agents may work either for both you and the buyers or just for the buyers alone.

Dual Agents

A dual agent is one who not only works for you the seller, but also works for the buyer. The dual agent represents both parties. The crux of a dual agent's responsibilities can be found, just as the seller's agent's could, in the price. A dual agent may not tell a buyer that you're willing to take less *and may not tell you that the buyer is willing to pay more.*

In other words, the dual agent, because he owes both you and the buyer loyalty, foregoes disclosing price information and other information, such as who's willing to concede terms, to either of you.

Buyer's Agent

Finally, there is the matter of an agent who works exclusively for the buyer. What's confusing is that this agent may also work from the listing sheet that your selling agent put your home on. However, this agent owes a fiduciary responsibility to the buyer. In the case of price, the buyer's agent is required to tell the buyer if she learns you are willing to take less, but is not required to tell you if the buyer is willing to pay more.

Thus there are in reality three separate levels of agent with corresponding duties:

Seller's (listing) agent—fiduciary to seller

Dual agent—fiduciary to buyer and seller

Buyer's agent—fiduciary to buyer

The real question is, how do you know with whom you're dealing? If you're dealing with your seller's agent, you can feel comfortable confiding everything, presuming the agent is honest and follows her fiduciary duties. On the other hand, if you're dealing with the buyer's agent, you should not confide anything, because every stray word that passes your lips will find its way back to the buyer. How do you know whom to trust?

Tip

Many sellers mistakenly believe that the payment of a commission determines the type of agent. For example, you pay the agent, therefore automatically the broker is a seller's agent. Not so. Many real estate regulating agencies including the California Real Estate Department have held that who pays the commission is irrelevant.

Agent's Disclosure

In the old days—several decades ago, the National Association of Realtors offered a code of ethics that was the forerunner of many of the rules of agency in most states. The code of ethics basically required that the agent deal fairly with all parties, both buyers and sellers.

This, however, was rather vague and left a great deal up to the interpretation (and imagination) of many agents. It is for that reason that today increasing numbers of states are requiring that agents disclose to you whom they represent.

Thus, when you sign your listing agreement, the agent may also present to you a second document which states, in effect, something like one of the following:

"I am a seller's agent with the following duties and responsibilities to you…and I have a duty to disclose to you all facts affecting the value of the property."

"I am a dual agent, and I represent both buyers and sellers. I may not disclose to you if a buyer is willing to pay more than the offered price."

"I am a buyer's agent, and I represent the buyer. I owe that buyer a fiduciary responsibility, and I may not disclose to you if a buyer is willing to pay more than the offered price."

Usually you must not only read the disclosure, but sign that you understand what it says. There's nothing wrong with signing—just be sure that you do, in fact, understand what it says.

Which Type of Agent Do You Want?

The question which arises out of all of this is which kind of agent do you want? The answer is simple, when you're selling your house you want only a seller's agent. You want to be sure that the person with whom you list will represent you thoroughly.

That's all well and good. But what happens when your agent goes out and brings in a buyer with no other agent involved. Does your agent now become a dual agent?

Maybe. It all comes out in disclosure. The agent who brings you the offer on your house should disclose what type of agent he is. If he doesn't disclose, you should demand a disclosure.

Tip

Whenever an offer is presented, demand to know who is represented by the agent presenting the offer. The agent should tell you. If the agent doesn't, presume that person is acting for the buyer and treat it as an adversarial offer. Keep a tight lip and don't blab what you might take, if it's less than is being offered.

The point to understand here is that the agent determines whom he represents. Your goal is to find out who it is, and then act accordingly.

Your Listing Agent's Responsibilities

In addition to the fiduciary responsibility of the agent, there's also the matter of selling your home. You sign a listing agreement with an agent in which you commit to pay that agent a large fee for bringing you a buyer. What does that agent commit to you in return? What is the agent bound to do?

In most cases questions of this sort arise after the home has been listed for a couple of months. With few to no buyers coming by, you're getting anxious. You're beginning to wonder if you chose the right agent after all. You look in the paper and you don't see your home advertised. Your agent isn't holding an "open house" in your home. What's she doing? Your question is born out of frustration.

Your next question is probably, what is your agent supposed to be doing? Is she not living up to her responsibilities and duties? Your final question is likely to be, what can I do about it? We'll deal with these questions here.

What Is Your Agent Supposed to Do for You?

Basically, your agent is supposed to sell your home. How he does that, in general, is up to the agent. As noted in earlier chapters, specifically advertising your property and holding "open houses" in it, per se, are no guarantee of buyers. Remember, buyers rarely purchase the home they see in the ad or visit on their own.

The part that the agent can do best, talking up your home to other agents, you will never get a chance to see. Thus, most of what your agent does for you, you have little to no control over. The best you can do is to "hire" a good agent and hope.

Some sellers insist on writing into their listing agreements that the agent will spend $\$x$ on advertising. The hope is that if the agent commits to a large enough figure for advertising the property, then he will push the property.

Maybe that works and maybe not. Most good agents I know won't agree to a set advertising figure. They know that it's money wasted and it reduces their commission. In the end, the agent who agrees to spending a set figure on advertising may not be the best agent to sell your property.

Tip

A good agent has an ethical responsibility to keep you informed at all times. That means that the agent calls you weekly to let you know what has been done to sell your home. This is not only good business practice, but it also may help with the sale since during those conversations you may be able to suggest sales approaches that the agent didn't think of. If your agent doesn't call you frequently, call your agent and demand to know what's going on.

What Can You Do If Your Agent Isn't Working for You?

This question almost never arises until at least a month has passed—usually during the second month of the listing. Until then, most sellers are filled with hope, even if no one comes by to see the house.

However, if the agent doesn't call, no buyers come by, there are no ads in the paper, and time is going by, you are very likely to get frustrated and angry. About this time most sellers call that darn agent and give her a piece of their minds.

This accomplishes two things. It makes the seller feel temporarily better, and it makes the agent angry and even less likely to work hard on the sale of the house. Thus, yelling at your agent isn't often going to produce the desired results.

But what can you do?

1. Determine if your agent really isn't working. Call or go to see your agent, and instead of showing anger, show concern. Explain that you haven't seen any results, and results, after all, are what listing and selling are all about. Give the agent an opportunity to explain, and listen carefully to the explanation.

Does it make sense? Was the agent just too busy to call you? Has a plan been put into effect to sell your property? Has the agent talked it up?

Remember, a good agent will always find time to call and keep you informed. It would take an extraordinary set of circumstances to keep a good agent from not talking to you.

2. Give the agent a second chance. If you are near the beginning or middle of the listing period, give the agent another two weeks. See what happens.

3. If after a second chance the agent still refuses to work on your property, demand to have your listing back.

Trap

When you sign a listing for a set period of time, generally speaking you cannot take back your listing unless the agent agrees. Some listing agreements contain a "liquidated damages" clause. Beware of this clause. It usually states that if for any reason you decide to take your house off the market, you owe the agent whatever fee was written in there.

Getting Out of Your Listing

There are many reasons that a seller wants to get out of the listing. Perhaps he has found someone he can sell the house to without the agent and he wants to avoid paying a commission. Or perhaps he's had an offer to rent the property. These are common reasons. However, when a seller hires an agent and agrees to an Exclusive Right to Sell listing, the seller gives up the right to sell or lease during the listing period without the agent's consent. Quite frankly, if the seller insists on breaking the agreement, the agent is entitled to a part if not all of the commission.

Good Reasons

On the other hand, there are other reasons for wanting to get out of a listing. The seller or a member of the immediate family may have become ill, the seller could have lost his or her job, the house could have partly burned down. These are all excellent reasons for getting out of a listing, and in almost all cases, the agent will readily agree. If the agent refuses, go to the local real estate board—they should be sympathetic and should apply pressure on the agent.

Judgment Calls

Then there is the middle ground. This is when you, the seller, feel the agent hasn't done any work and hasn't lived up to the listing agreement. The last time you saw or heard from the agent was when you signed the listing. There has been no sign in the yard, no advertising, and as far as you can tell, the agent hasn't talked up your property. Maybe the agent even left on vacation as soon as you signed up. Your house isn't selling while others are. You want out so you can try selling it yourself or so you can get a different agent.

When you finally get hold of your agent, she says that she has worked on your listing as hard as she could, and she refuses to give it up.

If you take this to the local real estate board, you're unlikely to get a sympathetic hearing. After all, who really is to say what constitutes working with diligence on a listing? Therefore, what can you do to get out of your listing?

Putting Pressure on Your Agent to Release Your Listing

1. If your agent is a salesperson, tell him that you are going to complain to the broker. If this doesn't do any good, go to see the broker and state your case. The broker may or may not be sympathetic depending on whether or not that broker thinks you are justified in your thinking.

2. Tell your agent that you are quite angry and that you are going to file a *written* complaint with the local real estate board and the state real estate licensing department. Quite frankly, since it's a matter of judgement, neither of these is likely to produce much in the way of results. But most agents would rather not have letters of complaint registered against them. If this doesn't move the agent, send the letters with a copy to the agent.

3. Tell the agent you're going to complain in writing to the local Chamber of Commerce, Better Business Bureau, even the district attorney. If the agent doesn't become agreeable to what you want, send the letters. Again, since it's a judgment call, don't expect big results.

4. Tell your agent you're going to write a letter of complaint to your local newspaper. This is a no win situation for the agent. Your complaint in the letters-to-the-editor department is going to draw public attention to the problem. This is a powerful tactic. If you've already said you were going to send letters (as described earlier), and then did, the agent will surely believe that you'll send this one. And who knows what letters local newspapers, which are traditionally hungry for news to fill

their pages, will print. If the agent doesn't go along, send the letter—just be sure that your letter states *facts* and does *not* contain any slander or libelous statements.

Notice that all of these tactics have two parts. First you tell the agent what you are going to do and give him a chance to respond. Then you do it. They also follow in sequence from lesser to greater pressure.

The point is that in reality, there's probably nothing specific that you can do. All that you can hope for is to convince the agent that you're sufficiently mad about what the agent has or has not done, that it's easier and better to just give back the listing.

What happens if your agent is a real stinker and isn't moved by any of it? Well, chances are you didn't really get upset until you were six weeks into the listing anyway. It's probably taken you four more weeks to accomplish all of the above, in another two weeks the listing should expire if it's just for three months. You'll just have to wait.

7

Your Disclosure Duties and Obligations

I'm sure you've heard the old story about the reluctant patient. It's worth repeating, however, because of its applications to real estate.

The reluctant patient went into the doctor's office and was quite obviously suffering greatly. The sympathetic doctor asked the patient to get up on the examining couch and then to lie prone. When the patient complied, the doctor asked, "Now, what's wrong?"

To which the patient replied, "You're the doctor—You tell me!"

While such an attitude is ludicrous in medicine, and therefore somewhat humorous, it is downright dangerous in real estate. Yet, it still prevails to a large degree in the minds of many sellers.

An agent comes in and asks if the property has any defects, and the sellers either say, "None that I know of," when they surely know of some. Or the buyer asks, "Any problems with the house?" to which the seller replies, "Nope," while muttering under his breath, "You're buying it...you find out!"

In the past, sellers generally got away with such an attitude because the prevailing legal and moral perspective was "caveat emptor," let the buyer beware. But today we live in an age of consumerism. Today, a cavalier attitude by the seller can have dire consequences.

Consequences of Failing to Disclose Problems

I recently had occasion to witness a confrontation between sellers, buyers, and agent that most certainly would not have taken place ten or perhaps even five years ago. The situation was quite simple on the face of it.

The buyers had purchased a single-family home in what appeared to be a nice neighborhood. They had paid close to asking price and the deal went smoothly. At the closing buyers, sellers, and agent all seemed satisfied. The deed was recorded in favor of the buyers, and the sellers received their cash out, the agent her commission.

About two weeks later the buyers called their agent and complained that there was a severe problem with the home. The next door neighbors had a teenage daughter and son who would play their stereo loud during the day and then have parties two or three times a week until early in the morning. The buyers weren't able to sleep or to enjoy their property. They said they had talked to the neighbors, all to no avail.

The agent chuckled and said that kids would be kids and to ignore it. If it got really bad, they should call the cops.

A week later the agent got another phone call. The buyers had called the police, who indicated that there wasn't much they could, or were willing to do and revealed that the former owners, the sellers, had frequently called to complain about the same thing. The buyers said they were thinking about demanding a rescission of the deal.

This caught the agent's attention. Rescission essentially means going back in time on a deal until all the parties are where they were before the deal was made. In other words, it means taking back the sale of the property.

The agent investigated and talked to the former sellers. The neighbors had indeed been a big problem. That, it turns out, was the real reason they had decided to sell. They had filed numerous police reports against those neighbors.

"But," the agent protested, "Why didn't you tell me about that? Why didn't you tell the buyers?"

"Because," came the reply, "Who would have bought the house if we'd mentioned it?"

The agent suspected she was in big trouble. She went to see the neighbors who were intransigent. They refused to curb their children.

She went to see the buyers, who had dark hollows under their eyes and who were in the process of contacting an attorney. They couldn't sleep, and if they couldn't sleep they were not getting the "quiet enjoyment" they were entitled to from their home. The agent had to agree.

The sellers did get an attorney and pursued the matter, although it never got to court. They discovered that in their state the seller's duty to disclose defects in the house to buyers was clear and enforceable. The seller had been negligent in not disclosing that there were bad neighbors. Thus the sellers (and the agent) were at fault.

How was it resolved? In the end the agent negotiated with the noisy neighbors to sell their home. Half the agent's fee for the second sale and half the neighbor's moving costs were paid by the sellers who hadn't disclosed. The other half of the two fees were paid by the agent.

It could have been much worse for the seller. The buyers might have insisted on rescission, in which case the seller might have had to pay back all the buyer's money, take back the house, and be subject to damages as well.

And it was all over noisy neighbors, something that wasn't directly a part of the house that was sold.

In recent years sellers have been held liable for a whole bundle of potential drawbacks to property that a decade ago would never have caused a raised eyebrow. These include:

A death or murder which occurred in the house being sold

A landfill nearby

Flooding, grading, or drainage problems

Zoning violations

Soil problems

Bad neighbors

And a host of other potential problems

All of which is to say that if you don't disclose problems with your property, the consequences could be severe.

It's What You *Should* Know That Counts

But, you may be saying to yourself. Those sellers in the example lied. I would never lie. I would simply reveal everything I knew about the house.

Unfortunately, it's like getting a traffic ticket. Ignorance of the law is no excuse. It's not always what you know and disclose to the buyers that counts. It's what you should have known and should have disclosed.

Much of the disclosure precedent came from a lawsuit in California

(*Easton* v. *Strassburger*, A010566, California First District Court of Appeal, February, 1984). The results of this lawsuit were codified in California law and subsequently in the real estate code of many other states. The California real estate code deals primarily with agents' responsibilities and states, "An agent's duty to prospective purchasers of residential property of one to four units is: to state that he or she has conducted a reasonably competent and diligent visual inspection of the listed property and to disclose all facts revealed that materially affect the value or desirability of the property."

With regard to the sellers, the rules can be even stricter. The sellers must disclose to the buyers any defects in the property that would materially affect its value or desirability in many cases whether or not the sellers are aware of those defects.

"But," I'm sure many readers are frothing, "how you can you disclose what you don't know?" The answer is simple, you can either conduct an inspection yourself, or you can hire a competent inspector (discussed at the end of this chapter).

Trap

Most of the problems with a home that a seller doesn't know anything about have to do with the various systems—plumbing, heating, electrical, gas, etc., as well as structure. You might live in a house for ten years and be totally unaware that a problem exists in the gas system. A buyer could purchase the home and it might blow up the next week. It could be argued that you should have had an inspection of the gas system to protect the buyer.

What Should You Inspect?

There are certain areas of the home that sellers should be aware of and that should be inspected either by you or a competent inspector. These include, but are not limited to the following:

1. Fireplace and fireplace exhaust—Loose bricks, blockage, chimney lining.
2. Electrical system—Circuit breakers, wall receptacles, switches, wiring, light fixtures, adequacy of grounding.
3. Heating/cooling system—Combustion chamber and cleanliness of heater, blockages, compression in air conditioner, motors, etc.
4. Plumbing—Type of pipe and age, rusting, leaks, water disposal condition, water pressure (too high or too low), etc.

5. Sewerage, septic tank, and other waste disposal (leakage, breakage, and blockage).

6. Foundation and structure—Cracks, breaks, leaning, flooding in basement.

7. Additions made without building department approval—Room additions, window or door changes, etc.

8. Exterior and roof—Age of exterior and roof and their condition, gutters and downspouts, cracking of stucco, peeling of paint.

9. Doors and windows (including leakage stains)—Weather stripping, hinges, alignment.

10. Drainage and flooding—Slope, groundwater conditions, drainage away from house.

11. Interior—Condition of walls, ceilings, carpets, and drapes.

12. Lot—Including safety of fences, gates, and any obstructions.

13. Appliances—Age and condition.

The Difference Between Disclosure and Warranty

While you must disclose problems and defects in your home, you don't necessarily have to fix them, unless they are a safety hazard. For example, your lot could have a perennial drainage problem. Every winter the storms in the nearby hills drop several inches of rain that floods your back yard. It lasts for about a week and then drains away. The buyers could be made *fully aware* of the problem and still purchase the house with the existing condition. You could be near a land fill that occasionally produces noxious smells. As long as the buyer is made fully aware of the problem and agrees to buy the house with it, you may complete the sale without making any corrections. What, for example, could you do about the landfill?

Of course, deciding the difference between what must be fixed and what needn't be fixed could be the job of a Solomon. However, one thing is clear: the more you disclose to a buyer, the less chance there is for you to have trouble later on.

Tip

To avoid even the suggestion of a problem, many sellers go out of their way to make disclosures about their homes to buyers. The idea is that the more you get out on the table before the sale, the less you have to worry about afterward.

To help sellers with their disclosures, agents and some real estate associations have created disclosure sheets that they give to sellers. If you're not using an agent, you can usually get a copy from an agent. These are given to prospective buyers and they help the sellers organize their disclosures. The sample disclosure statement shown on pages 77 and 78 illustrates the kind of information that such a statement typically contains.

When to Disclose

It's important to understand that to avoid any possibility of problems, you should disclose defects or problems with your house as soon as possible. That means *before* the buyer makes an offer. In other words, if you're using an agent, the agent should present your disclosure sheet to the buyer before taking an offer. If you're handling the house yourself, you should present it to the buyer before accepting any money or signing any sales agreement.

Be sure that the disclosure sheet is made at least in duplicate and that you retain a copy signed by the buyers stating that they have seen and had a chance to read it.

Trap

If you wait until after the buyer makes an offer you accept to show the disclosure sheet the buyer may have the right to take back the offer.

House Inspections

What should be apparent from this discussion is that you need to know a great deal about your house when you sell it, usually far more than the average seller knows or wants to know. So, how do you handle disclosure without spending the next six months learning about construction?

Many sellers use an inspector. The inspector solves a whole series of problems. If the inspector you use is bonded, and a problem arises after the sale, it is easy enough to say to the buyers, "I didn't know there was a problem. I had the house inspected and I trusted the word of the inspector. Blame the inspector."

Occupancy

Who is occupying the property?_____

If it's a tenant, will there be any difficulties in getting possession?

_____

_____

Appliances and features contained in the house

(*Note*: The following is only a partial checklist)

Oven	[ ]	Trash compactor	[ ]
Range	[ ]	Microwave	[ ]
Dishwasher	[ ]	Washer/dryer hookups	[ ]
Sewer	[ ]	Septic tank	[ ]
TV antenna	[ ]	Security system	[ ]
Well	[ ]	Wall air-conditioners	[ ]
Sprinklers	[ ]	Solar heating	[ ]
Gutters	[ ]	Fire alarm	[ ]
Intercom	[ ]	Gazebo	[ ]
Spa	[ ]	Carport	[ ]
Garage	[ ]	Garage door opener	[ ]
Pool	[ ]	Heater/filter	[ ]
Window screens	[ ]	Satellite dish	[ ]
Exhaust fan	[ ]	Garbage disposal	[ ]
Fireplace	[ ]	220 volt wiring	[ ]

Other (list)

_____

_____

Roof

Age _____

Type _____

Condition _____

Defects or problem areas in the house

Interior walls	[ ]	Exterior walls	[ ]
Ceilings	[ ]	Floors	[ ]
Roof	[ ]	Insulation	[ ]
Windows	[ ]	Doors	[ ]

Foundation	[ ]	Slab	[ ]
Driveway	[ ]	Sidewalk	[ ]
Fences	[ ]	Gates	[ ]
Electrical	[ ]	Plumbing	[ ]
Sewer	[ ]	Heating/cooling	[ ]
Structure	[ ]		

Other problem areas

1. Is there a homeowner's association?

2. Are there any common areas? Describe them.

3. Are there any lawsuits which might affect the property?

4. Any deed restrictions or other CC&R restrictions?

5. Any bond obligations (such as a bond to pay for a sewer connection)?

6. Any zoning or setback violations?

7. Any damage to the property from fires?

8. Any damage from flooding or earthquakes?

9. Any settling or soil slippage?

10. Any room additions made without building permit?

11. Any encroachments from neighboring properties?

12. Any easements?

13. Any landfill on the property?

14. Any common fences or driveways shared with neighbors?

15. Any other problems with the property?

Note: The above disclosure statement is not to be used as is from the book, but is designed to be used for comparison purposes with the disclosure statement given to you by your attorney or agent.

That, of course, doesn't get you off the hook, but it does help things. In addition, if there are damages to be paid and the inspector is to blame and is bonded, the inspector may have to pay them instead of you.

Thus, using an inspector can be very worthwhile.

Finding a Reputable House Inspector

Almost anyone can inspect a house. I can inspect your house; you can inspect mine. But does that mean that either one of us is qualified? Not at all.

In recent years contractors, particularly those who aren't having a terrific year, have taken to house inspections as a way of raising additional money. A house inspection typically costs between $250 and $300 as of this writing. A contractor can walk through your house, put checks on a form, and pick up several hundred dollars for a few hours work. It's not surprising that many are doing it.

But are contractors qualified? Some are and some aren't. A contractor who builds new houses may not know a great deal about old houses. A plumbing contractor may not know about electrical. A cement contractor may know very little about roofs. The value of their inspections may be questionable.

The real problem is that housing inspections are relatively new. In a few years states will undoubtedly begin licensing and testing housing inspectors. But as of now, few if any states are doing this, so sellers are on their own.

One way of qualifying a potential house inspector is to insist that this person be a member of ASHI. This is the American Society of Home Inspectors. It is a trade organization which has been endeavoring to raise the standards of house inspectors in general. Figure 7-1 is a home inspection illustration (provided by ASHI).

ASHI sets standards for inspectors and makes an effort to see that its membership follows those standards. ASHI, however, does not require its members to be contractors. Personally, I don't think that having a contractor's license necessarily qualifies a person as a house inspector. For more information about ASHI you can contact the organization at Suite 630, 1010 Wisconsin Ave., NW, Washington, D.C. 20007. Their number is (202) 842-3096.

Trap

Beware of contractors who offer to do a home inspection for a nominal fee, then find something wrong and offer to fix it, usually for a high

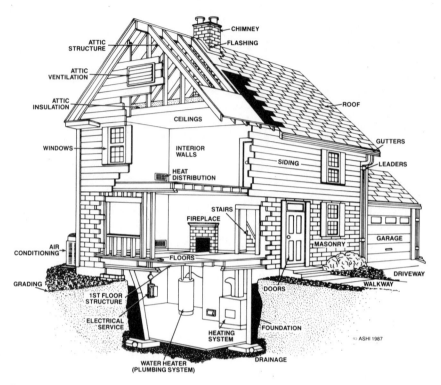

CHIMNEY
FLASHING
ATTIC STRUCTURE
ATTIC VENTILATION
ATTIC INSULATION
ROOF
CEILINGS
WINDOWS
INTERIOR WALLS
GUTTERS
SIDING
LEADERS
HEAT DISTRIBUTION
STAIRS
FIREPLACE
AIR CONDITIONING
MASONRY
GARAGE
FLOORS
GRADING
DRIVEWAY
WALKWAY
DOORS
1ST FLOOR STRUCTURE
ELECTRICAL SERVICE
HEATING SYSTEM
FOUNDATION
(c) ASHI 1987
WATER HEATER (PLUMBING SYSTEM)
DRAINAGE

Figure 7-1

fee. Some unscrupulous contractors have been using home inspection as a way of procuring business. A good rule of thumb is to never have the person do the work who does the inspection. Also, don't ask the inspector to refer you to someone. That someone could be the inspector's brother-in-law or sister who is in on the scam.

Tip

Always insist on getting a written report from an inspector. An oral report is useless to you if there should be a problem from the buyer later on. When problems occur, everyone seems to remember things differently. You may say the inspector told you the house was perfect, but the inspector may say that the defects that the buyer is now complaining about were certainly pointed out.

Get it in writing.

Termite Inspection

This is just a quick note to point out that termite inspections are not really a new part of the home inspection process. Lenders have been requiring termite inspections as a condition for approving a new home loan for decades. A termite inspection and the repair of damage has been a requirement of home sales almost as long. In almost all states termite inspectors are licensed, and their written reports are required to be registered.

Home Warranties

In addition to an inspection, you can also obtain a home warranty which covers the major systems (heating, electrical, plumbing, etc.) as well as appliances. The home warranty usually costs about $300 a year, with the seller paying the first year, and may be money well spent. Contact an agent for home warranty companies available in your area.

8

What to Do
If Your House
Won't Sell

Sometimes sellers have problem houses. You put the home up for sale, and for whatever reason, the property doesn't sell. This can be one of life's more frustrating situations. It can lead to indigestion, problems at work, and even marital strife.

A lot of the frustration associated with problem houses has to do with anticipation. You decide to list or to sell FSBO and look forward to a sale within a "reasonable" time. What's reasonable? For most people it's within a month or two. If it takes longer, fears begin to creep in that maybe the house won't sell, maybe there's something wrong with it, maybe you'll have to lower the price. There are a lot of maybes possible, and when you have anticipated that your home is going to sell and it doesn't, they all come to mind.

The first thing that you should do when your house doesn't sell as fast as you hoped it would is to dump those fears. Yes, you can sell your house. There are lots of things that can be done to make a sale. Ultimately, there is almost no house that can't be sold unless the market is truly terrible. If other houses are selling, yours can be sold too.

What you have to do is to stand back and analyze the situation. Find out what's causing the problem and take steps to correct it. That's what we're going to do in this chapter.

Why Isn't It Selling?

There are generally seven reasons that a house won't sell. They are:

Time

Exposure

Market

Neighborhood

Condition

Price

Terms

While many of these reasons for not selling are related, for simplicity we'll consider each separately.

Time

If your home isn't selling, perhaps its because you just haven't given it enough time. Remember that the amount of time that it takes to sell a home differs with each property. Perhaps you went to a local agent and discovered that the average time to sell a home in your area was 55 days. So, you assumed your home would sell within two months. Two and a half months have gone by and it hasn't sold. What happened?

Perhaps something is indeed wrong, and you should check out the other causes for not selling listed below. But, assuming that nothing's amiss, perhaps you just have to give it more time. Remember, to sell a house you need only one buyer, but, like fishing, you have to wait for that buyer to get hooked.

Tip

As a rule of thumb, add 50 percent to the average time it takes to sell a house in your area. For example, if it takes two months, on the average, to sell a home, give yourself three. Don't panic until the end of the third.

Exposure

Lack of exposure simply means that not enough buyers have been made aware of the fact that your home is for sale. There are several ways of tracking exposure.

1. *Count the number of buyers who come through looking at your house.* This is the easiest method. You can count heads or you can have a little sign-in book. If you haven't had a visit from a buyer in several weeks, it's a bad sign. On the other hand, if buyers keep coming through and looking and there are no offers, you may have a problem with price or terms.

2. *Count the number of real estate people who come through.* Assuming you have your house listed, you should have "caravans" of agents coming through, particularly when it first goes on the market. Whole offices of agents, who are now aware your property is listed, will come by to see it, to remember it, and to determine if they have any buyers for it. Later, individual agents will come by seeing if your house is right for a particular buyer they have.

Each time an agent comes by they leave their business card. Count the cards. If there are only a few, it could mean trouble. Agents know that they can't see all of the houses for sale, thus they only pick out the most likely ones. Few business cards means they may be avoiding your house. You could have a problem with price or neighborhood.

3. *Count the number of calls that you get.* If you're selling FSBO, you undoubtedly have a sign out and an ad in the paper. If you do, you're bound to get calls. If those calls don't come in or if there are very few of them or if the potential buyers who call are confused about what you're selling or hang up when you explain what you've got, you may have a problem. Recheck your advertising for clarity and impact.

Market

In an earlier chapter we discussed analyzing the market to see if it was hot, warm, cool, or cold. If you did such an analysis, perhaps you did it incorrectly or perhaps the market has changed.

If your reanalyze the market and are convinced that it's hot or warm, then look closely at other factors, particularly the condition of your home, the neighborhood, and the price.

On the other hand, if you discover that the market is cool or cold, then some reevaluation regarding the sale may be in order. In a cold market you may not be able to sell your home, regardless of how much time you spend trying, until the market turns around. In a very bad market, there simply aren't many buyers.

In a cool (bad) market, the first tendency is to try lowering the price to get buyers interested. However, while it's an economic truth that lowering the price far enough will eventually get someone interested, most sellers cannot lower their prices significantly because they have high mortgages. You're not going to sell your home for less than you've borrowed against it. So what do you do? In a cool market, you may have to be creative.

When Your House Won't Sell
Because the Market Is Cool

1. Offer creative financing.   If your current loan is assumable (FHA, VA), offer to carry back much of the down payment in the form of a second if the buyers assume the loan. In this way you can get a buyer in without qualifying and with very little cash.

Trap

Buyers who get in with little cash and no qualifying often have no loyalty if times get tough and they can't keep up the payments. They might simply walk away from the house. To protect your investment, you might have to foreclose on your second mortgage—an expensive and time consuming problem.

2. Rent your house.   The thing about bad markets is that they don't last forever. While it may be impossible to sell for what you have in your house, you may be able to rent it quite easily. (Of course, this assumes that you're moving.) Even if you have to rent it for just your payments…even if you have to rent it for a little less than your payments, you could then hang onto it and get through the rough times.

If you need the money from your home to purchase another, why not borrow it? If you have good credit, a lender may be more than willing to loan you most of your equity, and you can pay back the loan with the rent.

Eventually the market will turn around, and when it does, you can then put your home up for sale, successfully.

3. Offer a Lease-Option.   A lease option is where you, in effect, rent your house, except that the tenant has the option to buy it at a later date for a set price.

Many would-be buyers who don't have much cash or credit are looking for lease-options. Typically, under a lease-option the tenant pays a little more than market rent each month, and after a set period of time, a portion of the rent is applied toward the down payment.

Lease-options will often attract people and get your house rented or sold in a very cold market.

Trap

Be aware that lease-options are not panaceas. Typically when you first enter into one, things are wonderful. The tenant pays on time and is quite content. However, as time goes by, the tenant often begins to see that the chances of really buying the property are dwindling. Maybe the tenant has to come up with additional money when it's time to exercise the option, and there is no money available. Or perhaps the tenant has to refinance and realizes that, given credit problems, this is going to be impossible.

Once the tenant becomes disenchanted, rents come in late, the upkeep of the property slips, and your worries start all over again. This doesn't mean that lease-options are bad. It does mean that they aren't cure-alls.

Neighborhood

Everyone knows that the three biggest considerations when buying real estate are location, location, and location. However, you may think that your neighborhood is okay, only to realize that others don't feel the same way. For example, your neighborhood may have deteriorated during the time you've lived there and you haven't really noticed. Or a big lumber mill a mile away never bothered you, but it turns off potential buyers.

You'll know if the neighborhood is the problem because people will tell you. Agents will tell you. Home hunters who stop by will tell you, if you ask. Even some of your neighbors will tell you.

If it turns out that your house isn't selling because it's in a bad location, what can you do about it? The best thing you could have done was to have bought in a better neighborhood. However, having already bought in, the one thing you cannot do is to change your home's location. If there's a landfill nearby or a swampy river or a blighted area, you can't move your house somewhere else. You can, however, endeavor within certain limits to change the neighborhood. People who wanted to sell their homes but were unable to eventually got the Love Canal cleaned up. In southern California home owners got landfill dumps closed in several instances. In other cases, sellers have created local home-owner associations which have made efforts to clean up neighborhoods.

All of these things take time and effort; however, if you're willing, they can ultimately produce results for you in the form of a sale.

You can also do other things, such as lowering the price. A good comparison here is the case of automobiles in a used car lot. You walk in and, of course, look at all the shiny models, but your wallet is a bit slim that day and you ask the dealer if there might not be a less expensive car available.

The dealer leads you to the back of the lot where there is a row of cars in not-so-hot condition, at least appearance-wise. The dealer says they all run great, but they need a coat of paint. However, to compensate for their appearance, the dealer will knock down the price 10 percent and carry the financing.

Would you buy?

Many people will. Many people will buy in a worse neighborhood if they can get a better deal. In some cases they need the better deal in order to buy at all. In other cases they just like to get good deals. When the neighborhood is bad, lower the price and offer better terms. Do it gradually, until you reach a point where you find a buyer who's interested.

Trap

When you go to buy a new house after you sell, don't look for these kinds of "deals" in undesirable neighborhoods. No matter how much lower the price or how much better the terms, location must remain your number one consideration. Buy for less because of neighborhood, and later on you'll have to sell for less. In addition, price appreciation is always slower in the less desirable neighborhoods.

Condition

The first chapters in this book dealt with condition. Maybe you read them and felt that your home was in good condition, but, it hasn't sold and you're beginning to wonder. Now's the time to get an educated second opinion.

Call in your agent, or ask others who come by, how your house compares in condition with other similar homes on the market. Be aware that most people will hesitate to come right out and say that your place is a pit, out of a desire not to offend you. But nearly everyone will drop hints: "Your house is lovely, except for that swamp of a pool in the back yard." Or, "No problems, except the carpeting has all those spots." Or, "It looks great and will look even better once you get a new roof on." Or, "Nothing wrong with it that a new coat of paint won't fix."

Take these comments to heart. Very often others see the condition of property far clearer than the owner. As sellers, we tend to overlook the bad and exaggerate the good. Potential buyers are not nearly so generous.

Tip

Work on the "curb appeal" of your home. Real estate agents recognize a fact of life when dealing with buyers: "First impressions count most." If your house looks beautiful when potential buyers drive up and first see it, those buyers are going to be favorably inclined toward the house, even if it's not perfect on the inside. This is called "curb appeal."

On the other hand, if the buyers see that your house is a bit run down looking, it's drab, and the landscaping is pitiful, they're going to look askance at the house even if it's perfect on the inside. One of the best things you can do is to improve the curb appeal of your house. Drive by with friends or neighbors and ask them what they initially see about your house that they like and don't like. Agents can also provide good clues here. Then take corrective measures.

If your house isn't selling because of some problem with its condition, take heart. You're far better off than the poor soul who's house won't sell because of location. You can't change location, but you can change condition. Often minor cosmetic changes such as paint, new lawn, and shrubs can make a world of difference.

Discover the problem and correct it and you should be well on the way toward selling that house.

Price

We've already discussed price at length in terms of other problems. For example, you may want to lower the price to compensate for a bad neighborhood. But what if there are no other problems? What if the neighborhood is fine, the house is in good condition, the market's warm if not hot, you've had great exposure, and it's been available for plenty of time? What if the sole problem is the price?

The most obvious solution is to lower it. However, you may not want to do that. You may have calculated what you have put into the house and what you want to get out and, by God, you're not lowering your price.

If that's the case, then don't. The general rule in real estate is that you can sell any property for any price, *if you wait long enough.*

It's largely a function of inflation. A seller's asking $100,000 for his property, but agents tell him it's not worth more than $90,000. He tells the agents to take a flying leap and keeps his property for sale and on the market.

Eighteen months later a buyer walks in and offers him $98,000 cash. That's close enough, he says, and takes it. Has he shown all the nay-sayers?

Hardly.

If the rate of inflation was 6 percent, and if his property kept up with it, at the end of 18 months the $90,000 was worth about $98,000 in inflated dollars. Thus, the buyer offered him the same price—90,000 in dollars of a year and a half ago or 98,000 in today's dollars. They're equal. ($90,000 + 18 months @ 6 percent inflation = $98,000.)

Our seller could have gotten the same price by selling 18 months sooner and sticking the money in the bank at 6 percent.

The moral of this story is that it's no good being stubborn about price. The more stubborn you are, the better a chance you're going to hurt yourself.

Of course, that doesn't mean that you want to lower the price to where you're going to lose money. But most buyers are quite savvy about what they can get for their bucks at any given time. In order to sell you're going to have to keep your price competitive with other homes on the market.

Terms

Terms cause the most confusion in real estate transactions. They are also the area of greatest opportunity.

Tip

Almost all buyers are hung up on price. Almost no buyers understand yield or terms. If you're willing to let the buyer have his or her price, you can often cut a deal that is so favorable to you in terms that it's better than getting your price.

Many times price isn't the issue. The problem could be high interest rates. It has been estimated that each time the mortgage interest rate goes up 1 percent, another 15 to 20 percent of potential buyers are forced out of the market—they just can't make the payments. When rates go beyond 12 percent, as they have in the last decade on several occasions, the market begins to close down. At 13 or 14 percent, the market is virtually shut down.

If you're trying to sell in a high interest rate market, what can you do? You can offer attractive terms. Chances are there are plenty of buyers just dying to purchase, but they can't because they can't afford (can't qualify for) the high payments that high interest rates produce. You can offer such buyers lower payments.

How you do this depends on your current financing. If you have an assumable FHA or VA loan on the property, you can allow the buyer to take over your own low payments.

Most people, however, are not in that fortunate a position. Most people have a "conventional" (non-government guaranteed or insured mortgage) loan on their property with a "due-on-sale" clause. This clause simply means that when you sell, the loan either has to be paid off or, at the lender's discretion, the buyers may take it over at the then current higher interest rate.

The new buyers are going to have to get a new loan. But that doesn't mean that you can't still offer favorable terms. Depending on your equity, you can reduce the payments and thus encourage buyers to consider your property.

Reducing the Payments for Buyers

Let's say that you're selling your home for $100,000 and you have a $60,000 mortgage on it—your equity is $40,000. Normally the new buyers would get a new loan for 80 percent ($80,000), paying off your existing loan and giving you $20,000 from the new loan as well as $20,000 in cash.

$ 20,000 cash down

$100,000 price

$ 80,000 new first mortgage

$ 20,000 to you

$ 60,000 pay off existing loan

Naturally you hope to get your equity in the property (roughly $40,000) out in cash, less perhaps $8000 in closing costs. The trouble is that in the market you are in interest rates happen to be in the 12 percent range. There aren't many buyers available who can come up with the payments on a new $80,000 mortgage.

An $80,000 mortgage at 9 percent interest has payments of $644 a month. But the same loan at 12 percent interest has payments of $823 a month. The buyers for homes in your price range may not be able to afford or can't qualify for the extra $179 per month.

But, you can help them to qualify. Offer to carry back a second mortgage for $20,000. Make that mortgage very attractive by offering a low interest rate and *no payments* until it is paid back in three years.

I'm sure some readers are wondering about a no payment mortgage. All that means is that instead of making payments monthly, the entire mortgage, along with interest, is payable on the due date. If you're familiar with zero coupon bonds, it's somewhat similar.

You'll accept $20,000 down and carry a $20,000 mortgage with no payments. That means that the buyers only need to get a $60,000 first mortgage at 12 percent. The payments on this loan are roughly $617 a month. In other words, the payments are within the affordable range.

$ 20,000 cash down

$100,000 price

$ 20,000 second mortgage (no payments)

$ 60,000 first mortgage (low $617 payments)

Would a seller go for such a deal? You bet! The seller would be thrilled. There'd be no payments on the second for three years and, hopefully, by then interest rates would have dropped and the seller could refinance, paying off the second with a larger, lower interest rate first.

Tip

In today's market ARMs (Adjustable Rate Mortgages) provide help to buyers by offering low initial "teaser" rates. The above procedure can be combined with an ARM to produce an even lower mortgage payment for the buyer.

Other Terms

Depending on the buyers' needs, you may want to provide other terms. For example, you may want to modify your occupancy demands to allow a buyer to get in sooner or later. You could offer to rent back the property for six months to help a buyer. You could offer to take most of the down payment in paper (second or third mortgage) instead of cash.

Trap

Beware of indiscriminately accepting paper instead of cash as a down payment. The more paper and less cash you accept, the weaker your position. The reason, simply, is that the less cash the buyers put in the property, the less inclined they are to hang on to it if times get tough.

If for some reason they can't make the payments and default, your only recourse when you hold a second or higher mortgage is to foreclose. That's expensive. You could end up "buying" your house back for more than its selling price.

Here are some alternatives to consider when you have a house that just won't sell.

1. Give it more time.
2. Get a new agent.
3. Advertise it more heavily.
4. Offer creative financing.
5. Rent it out.
6. Give a lease-option.
7. Start a neighborhood-improvement group.
8. Get city or county help in cleaning up your neighborhood.
9. Start petitions to close landfills, obnoxious plants, and other detracting influences in the neighborhood.
10. Paint your house.
11. Fix up your yard.
12. Improve the curb appeal of your house.
13. Lower your price.
14. Carryback a second mortgage.
15. Offer a "no-payment" mortgage.

9

How to Negotiate the Sale

It's what you've been waiting for since you first decided to put your home on the market. All those weekends of painting and fixing up, those hours of research finding the right price to ask, the talking and consulting until you came up with just the right agent, or decided to sell FSBO—they've all paid off. You've got an offer!

Your agent called (or a buyer, if you're a FSBO) and said that he has gotten an offer. He's going to bring it by in just a short while. You're finally on your way out of this house and on to your next. You can hardly wait. At last it's over. The long ordeal has ended.

Wrong!

If you're like most sellers, your ordeal has just begun. When that agent or buyer comes over and you take a look at that offer, you'd better be sitting down. Unless you're in a hot market, the offer is likely to be for a price lower than you want to accept, and the terms are very likely to be onerous to you. In other words, the offer has every chance of being unacceptable.

Now, the real process of selling your house begins. You have to negotiate with the buyers in the hopes that you can get out of the deal at least what you feel you minimally need, and they, hopefully, will still want to purchase.

The negotiations, with counteroffers, often take a long time and can stretch into the wee hours of the morning. I've heard many sellers complain that the negotiations were the hardest, the most painful part of the entire sales procedure. One even moaned that it was worse than getting a tooth filled without anesthetic.

Our goal in this chapter is to take the pain out of negotiating and to get the best deal for you. Which brings up another issue. Should you have your attorney look over the offer? The answer is yes, if you want to be safe. The attorney can explain complex clauses and protect your position. Just be careful your attorney doesn't protect you so well that you lose the deal. Most agents cringe when they see an attorney is involved out of fear he or she will insist the deal so favor you that no buyer will agree.

Know Your Fallback Position

In any negotiations there are winners and there are losers. Often the losers don't even know they lost for days or weeks afterward. But the winners always know they won. The reason is simple: the winners define winning before they start.

In your case you must know what you will and will not accept before you begin negotiations. This means knowing before the agent sits down with you or before the buyer hands over the offer and says, "Let's talk."

If you're honest with yourself, you'll realize that the price you're asking for your home and the terms you're demanding are part realism and part hope. What you must now do is pare away the part that's hope. Let's say that houses like yours have been selling in the $60,000 to $65,000 price range. So you put your house up for $65,000. That's hope.

Now an offer's coming in. You've got to understand that to be realistic you might have to accept $60,000, maybe less. The question is, how much less are you willing to accept?

In reality, there's only one way to decide how much is the least amount you'll take for your home. You have to, at some point, say to yourself, "I'd rather not sell unless I get at least $x." You fill in the xs. That's your bottom price.

Tip

I believe it is an excellent exercise to try to determine in advance what the minimum acceptable offer you'll accept will be. However, keep in mind that it's one thing to imagine what is the minimum you'll accept, and quite another to be faced with losing a sale unless you accept just a little bit less. Unfortunately, you may not really find out how little you'll really take until you're actually faced with making the decision.

Go through the same exercise with terms. You will or will not accept seller financing. If you are going to give a second mortgage the minimum interest rate you'll accept is x percent. The maximum term is x years. And so on.

Know, or try to know, what your minimums are before you start the negotiations. If you can do that, you can't lose, since you won't take less than those minimums. This becomes your fallback position.

Psychological Warfare

Assuming that the offer is going to be presented by an agent, usually the buyer's agent as well as your agent, the seller's agent, will be present. You should be aware of the subtle pressures that can be brought to bear on you. Remember, after all, that neither agent gets a penny unless you agree to the offer.

In most cases where I've been present when an offer is being presented, the agent begins with a statement something like this, "I'm sure you'll agree with me that this is an excellent offer, probably the best offer that you can expect to get at this time. When you've had a chance to look it over thoroughly I'm sure you'll realize how generous the buyer has been."

You could be asking $200,000 and the buyer could be offering $100,000. You could be asking all cash and the buyer could be demanding that you carry 100 percent financing. Still, when it's presented, it always seems to be a "good" offer, the "best" offer, the "most favorable and generous" offer, and so on.

I once knew a very good agent who, when faced with presenting an offer that was far off the mark, would always begin by asking the sellers, "Are you creative people?" Most of us are hard pressed to answer that we're not creative. When the sellers would say, yes, the agent would continue, "I knew it. I knew you'd be willing to look at this offer with an open mind, because it's a creative offer."

The number of different ways to present an offer is enormous, but it all usually comes down to the same thing. The agent tries to get you into a good mood, a mood of acceptance, and then hits you with the troubles.

How to Receive an Offer

Most sellers have no idea how to receive an offer. In most cases they sit there dumbly while the agent puts a copy filled with clauses and tiny writing in front of them and then proceeds to read through it line by line, often obscuring some of the most salient points.

The correct way to receive an offer is to direct the proceedings. You take charge. Once in charge, you can quickly find out what the strong and weak points of the offer are, and then start making your decisions.

When the agent begins, "This is how I like to proceed..." interject the following comment: "This is my house and I want to proceed in the following manner." Then list what you want to know in the order of importance to you. Here's a handy list of items prioritized in the order you may wish to receive them:

Order for Receiving Information about the Offer

1. Deposit—How much and who has it. Is it a serious offer as evidenced by a sufficient deposit?

2. Price.

3. Down payment—Cash, or if not, why not?

4. Terms—New first loan.

5. Terms—Any seller financing.

6. Occupancy—How soon do I have to get out?

7. Any contingencies?

As you go through the above questions, be sure you understand them. When you don't understand something, ask for an explanation. If you still don't understand, don't be hesitant to ask to have it explained again and again. Only a fool is afraid to ask a question when his or her money is at stake. (If you still don't understand, get an attorney.)

Trap

Don't jump to conclusions. You may hear that the price is substantially lower than even your fallback position. The tendency is to throw up your hands and say, "No, never!"

This is a mistake. Even if the price is low, the terms may make up for it or vice versa. In any event, you never, never want to turn down an offer cold. Always make a counteroffer as described shortly.

How to Tell a Good Offer from a Bad One

If you've already prepared yourself with a fallback position, you'll know pretty quickly if the offer being presented is acceptable or not. If you haven't prepared a fallback position, then you're going to have to make some quick decisions.

Usually it's not an easy call. The buyer may give you some things you want in exchange for demanding others that you don't want to give up. For example, the buyer may give you your price, but insist on onerous terms such as a long-term mortgage carried back by you at a low interest rate. You have to decide if it's worth accepting such terms in order to get your price.

Or the offer may insist that you be out of the house within 30 days. But, you protest, the kids are in school. You need at least 90 days. The agent makes it quite clear that the buyers have to be in within 30 days because they're moving into the area in that time. The agent says they won't compromise. Do you want to sell enough to move twice, once to a rental, and a second time to your next home?

These are just a few of the trade-offs you may encounter. To help you make a decision, try the following decision-making procedure:

Decision Maker

Pros	Points	Cons	Points
1. _____	_____	1. _____	_____
2. _____	_____	2. _____	_____
3. _____	_____	3. _____	_____
4. _____	_____	4. _____	_____
5. _____	_____	5. _____	_____
Total	_____	Total	_____

List the pros and cons of the offer on this or a similar sheet. Of course, the assigning of points to issues is going to be arbitrary, and you may feel that it's silly to do it. If so, then at least consider listing the pros and cons so you can see what the trade-offs are. The use of points is just an attempt to quantify the issues so that you can see at a glance which are more important.

Contingency Clauses

In an offer a contingency clause (also sometimes called a "subject to" clause) is usually a bad word if you're a seller. A contingency clause means just what it says—the offer is contingent on something happening as described in the clause.

A contingency clause is normally hand-written into the offer and is an added condition—in addition to all the prepared boilerplate that's already part of the document. It often goes on the back of the document. Be very careful of contingency clauses

Trap

Contingency clauses are often misunderstood by sellers because they are written in instead of being part of the prepared form of the offer. Be sure you understand all the implications of the contingency clause before you accept or reject it. *If necessary, hold off making a decision on the offer until you've had your lawyer look at it and explain it to you.*

Typical Contingencies

The buyers will purchase contingent upon their selling their present home—a very weak offer.

The buyers will purchase contingent upon their getting new financing—if they're already qualified, perhaps an excellent offer.

The buyers will purchase contingent upon Uncle Tod's cow delivering a new calf—a frivolous offer.

Contingency clauses are ways for the buyers (and sometimes the sellers) to get out of the deal. When buyers insist on a contingency clause it's like telling you, "Yes we'll buy, maybe." It's the "maybe" that's the killer.

Your goal is to let as few of the buyer's contingency clauses as possible into the agreement and to limit those which are included by time and performance. Let's look at this more closely.

Limiting the Contingency Clauses

Smart buyers will put few contingency clauses into an agreement—foolish or nervous buyers put many. If you have many (more than two) in your offer to purchase, then you need to be particularly wary.

How do you handle contingency clauses? My suggestion is that you examine each one carefully and ask yourself three questions.

1. Is the contingency reasonable? (Making the purchase contingent upon getting financing is usually reasonable. Making it subject to Uncle Tod coming down and looking at the house in the next month or two, isn't.)

2. Does this contingency negate the value of the offer? (The buyers of-

fer all cash, contingent upon their final approval of the property sometime before closing—there's no deal here as the buyers can refuse the property at their option at any time.)

3. Can I live with the contingency or should I make a counteroffer.

Tip

Remember, the offer to purchase is just that—an offer. You're not compelled to accept. The offer has no binding affect on you until you sign. (Remember that the purchase offer can also be called the deposit receipt or the sales agreement.)

If the contingency is unreasonable, negates the value of the offer, or is something you can't live with, then you must take action. You may want to turn down the offer and make a counteroffer. Note, however, that this can cost you the deal, as explained below.

Making the Counteroffer

When an offer to purchase is presented to you, you really have only three choices.

1. You can accept it exactly as it is.

2. You can reject it.

3. You can reject it and then counter with an offer of your own.

Notice that *you cannot accept it and make changes in it.* As soon as you make any changes to the offer the buyers give to you, it's a rejection of that offer. You may, for example, like the offer, but the buyers want you out by the 20th, which is a Friday, and you change it to the 21st, which is a Saturday, and gives you more time to move. You've rejected the offer.

When you reject the buyers' offer, they have every right to simply walk away from the deal. They wanted the date to be Friday the 20th so they would have time to move. They won't budge. Besides, they've found a house they like more than yours, so they're not interested any more. You've lost the deal.

Tip

If you possibly can live with it, it's usually a good idea to accept the offer as it is presented. This assumes, of course, that the price, terms, and contingencies are all within your fallback parameters. In other words, if the deal is very close to what you want, you may be making a mistake by trying to get the last penny or the last favorable term. By going for everything you want with a counteroffer, you risk losing what otherwise may be a sure deal.

What Is a Counteroffer?

A counter is a separate, new offer. Only this time, instead of the buyers making an offer to you, you are making an offer to them.

This is somewhat confusing since many agents write the counter-offer right on the back of the original offer, adding language which states that, "Seller accepts offer with the following changes...," and then the changes are listed. The trouble is that it all sounds like you've accepted something.

In truth, you've rejected the offer and are presenting a new offer to the buyer. However, psychologically, many agents feel that if the new offer comes back on the same document and it appears that there are only a few changes, the buyers might be more willing to accept it. This is probably good psychology, although it makes for messy offers, particularly if the buyers then counter your offer.

The important thing to remember is that each time you counter and each time the buyers counter, it's a new offer, regardless of how similar to the old offers it may be. You may end up only $100 apart, but if one of you disagrees, there is no deal.

When to Counter

There's only one time to counter and that's when you can't accept the offer that's presented. In my opinion you should almost never reject an offer flat out without a counter. Simply saying no doesn't give the buyers an opening to come back. Maybe the first offer was tentative on their part. They were just seeing if you were desperate enough to sell at a ridiculously low price. Now they're ready to come back with a higher offer, but if you don't counter, they may feel you're unwilling to budge at all, that you're unreasonable and impossible to deal with. They may go elsewhere.

Tip

In a very hot market, some savvy sellers do reject offers for less than full price. They're assuming that, given the market, they should be able to get exactly what they are asking and the only way to convince a buyer of this is to give a flat-out rejection. I've seen this work, although you'd better be sure of your market before you try it.

A few years ago I was selling a small home in San Jose, California. It was a rental property, and I hadn't really seen it in a few years, although I did stop by just prior to putting it on the market to judge the condition and set a price that I thought was fairly reasonable. I listed it with a local broker for a price of $115,000.

Almost two months later the broker called to say that he had an offer. When I got together with the agents, a seller's broker and a buyer's broker, I discovered that while the terms were acceptable, the offer was for $97,000, considerably less than I thought the property was worth.

The buyer's agent pointed out that this and that were wrong with the property, that it had been a rental and had been beaten up, and that $97,000 was all that it was worth. My seller's agent sat quietly and never commented. When I asked for his advice, he said, "Better take it. It's the first offer in nearly two months."

Both agents advocated the offer. However, having examined the market and the house, I considered the offer frivolous. While the property might not bring the full $115,000 I was asking, it surely should bring something close.

I was tempted to simply reject the offer out-of-hand, since the offering price and my asking price were so far apart. However, instead I counteroffered. I countered at $114,000, $1000 less than my asking price.

My reasoning was that the offer was frivolous: someone trying to steal the property for nothing. If that were the case, I would never hear from the buyers again. Or, it was a serious offer from a buyer who wanted to know how desperate I was to sell.

To my amazement, the buyer re-countered at $113,000, up $16,000 from the previous offer and within $2000 of my original asking price. I accepted.

The moral here is that you as a seller never know what buyers are thinking and unless you give buyers the benefit of the doubt with a counteroffer, you could be passing up an otherwise good deal.

How to Counteroffer Effectively

There are usually four areas in which you may want to make a counter offer:

Price

Terms

Occupancy

Contingencies

Remember, however, that if you make a counter in even just one of these areas, you've rejected the buyers' offer and they may decide, on second thought, that they want to change some of the other areas.

Price

This is usually the number one concern for both buyers and sellers. Yes, you want and should get your price. Just remember, however, that the buyers feel the same way.

Trap

Beware of a little game that sometimes occurs with offers. It's called, "split-the-difference." In this game someone offers you less than you're asking. For example, you're asking $100,000 and they offer you $90,000. Since you had thought to get only $95,000 out of the deal anyhow, you decide to split-the-difference and counter at $95,000.

Now, however, the buyers decide to split-the-difference again and they counter at $92,500. What are you going to do? If you split the difference again, you're going to counter at $93,750, less than your fallback position. If you reject the offer flat out, you may lose the deal. Splitting-the-difference has done you in.

It's important never to reveal your rock-bottom price. If the buyers offer less than you're asking, perhaps you may want to counter at a price lower than you were originally asking, but still higher than your rock-bottom price so that you can still have some maneuvering room.

Terms

This is where you might have the greatest flexibility. Most often the buyers are seeking a new loan and plan to pay cash down to the loan. But many times they are asking you to carry part of the financing, perhaps a second or third mortgage for a portion of the down payment.

Just remember that everything is negotiable here. If you're willing to carry back some of the financing, you may agree to their proposed terms, but change the length of the loan or the interest rate. The shorter the mortgage and the higher the interest rate, generally speaking, the better the deal for you.

Tip

If you carry back "paper" (a second or higher mortgage), try to see that it includes a monthly payment at least equal to the interest owed and that it also includes a late penalty for failure to make the payment on time. This will often make the mortgage more saleable should you decide at a later date to cash it in. (See the chapter on seller financing.)

Occupancy

Although it seems a simple thing, I've seen more deals fall apart because of a disagreement over occupancy than anything else. You need to stay, the sellers need to get in, and neither will budge...the deal goes south.

If you want to sell your home, you have to be prepared to be flexible in terms of the timing. You have to be willing to give up on your schedule, if it means making the deal.

I've seen sellers move out early and live in a motel or rented house in order to make a deal. I've seen sellers stay six months longer than they planned, and pay rent to the buyers, because the buyers couldn't get in right away. I've even seen sellers give the buyers a bonus if they would agree to wait a few months extra before moving in.

There is really no reason an occupancy problem should ruin a deal, as long as you're flexible. Here are some alternatives:

1. Change your own time plans.
2. Move and rent for a while.
3. Stay and rent from the buyers.
4. Pay buyers a bonus to change their plans.
5. Rent a motel for the buyers until you can move out.

Think of it this way. Is it worth a little inconvenience to sell your house?

Contingencies in the Counteroffer

In the counteroffer there are two ways to handle an unwanted contingency clause—the straightforward approach and the diplomatic approach.

Being Straightforward. Simply cross out the contingency. You won't accept it. This states your position clearly, but, it may offend the buyer and cost you a deal.

Tip

I had a very successful builder friend who had an absolute rule regarding contingencies—he refused to sign any agreement with a contingency in it, no matter how innocuous the clause was. It's something to remember.

Being Diplomatic. Limit the contingency. The buyers have inserted a contingency which says that the purchase is subject to a great aunt coming down and approving the bedroom she'll be living in when the house is purchased. Fine. Accept the contingency only add that the great aunt has to give her approval within 48 hours.

You haven't insulted the buyers. You haven't suggested that the contingency was a ploy to allow them to get out of the deal. You've gone along with it. You've agreed to take your house off the market for two days while the buyers satisfy the great aunt or who ever.

But, you've also made it clear that you mean business and that you don't have time for frivolous antics. After 48 hours they either remove the contingency or they lose the house.

Time is an excellent limiter of contingencies.

Or the buyers say they want a structural engineer to examine your home to be sure that the last earthquake (you live in California) hasn't damaged it. Instead of simply saying, no, you won't do that (which only makes the buyers' suspicious), agree...provided that they pay for the inspector and that they approve it within one week.

This time you've limited the contingency by action and time.

Limiting the contingencies makes it appear that you're going along with the buyers' wishes all the while making the offer more acceptable to you.

Removing the Contingency

Also, if you're limiting a contingency by time, be sure that you specify how that contingency is to be removed. For example, the sellers want a soil inspection to check for drainage and flooding. You agree, but specify that they must provide you with written approval of a completed report within, for example, a week, otherwise the deal is off.

Tip

___

Contingencies work both ways. There may come a time when you want to add a contingency to your benefit. For example, the buyers want you to supply a termite clearance, which is pretty standard and usually a necessary part of getting a new loan. But, you're afraid that there might be extensive termite damage. You don't mind spending a few hundreds bucks to clean up the termites, but you might balk at spending a few thousand. You might write in a contingency that limits your costs in supplying the clearance to, say, $1000. If it's more than that amount, the deal's off. Be careful that when you signed your listing agreement you didn't already agree to a termite clearance regardless of the costs.

Desperation Offers

What do you do when you've been too clever? The buyers made an offer, you countered at higher than your fallback position, but lower than your asking price fully expecting the buyers either to accept or to counter back. But instead, the buyers have done nothing. Apparently they are simply rejecting your offer. Does that mean the deal is dead?

Not necessarily. There is nothing to keep you from making a second counteroffer even though the buyers have rejected the first and have not countered back.

Of course, it puts you in a rather silly and weak position. You counter $66,000 for example, and when the buyers flat out refuse, you counter $64,000. It's bound to make the buyers wonder just how low you'll go if they just hang tight.

Tip

___

When making desperation counters, I believe a good rule of thumb is to only make *one*. Tell the buyers, through the agent if possible, that you really want to sell and that you hoped that they would counter. However, since they didn't, you're going to make them one last, final offer— your very best deal so to speak. Make it perfectly clear that this is your fallback position offer. If they don't take it, there won't be any others forthcoming. Sometimes it works. Of course, it raises this question, what if the buyers now counter at lower than your fallback position? (Selling real estate can be so aggravating!)

Ultimately, as always, you have to decide what is the minimum for which you'll sell your property. You can't go any lower than you can go.

What Happens When You Accept an Offer?

You don't accept an offer until you sign the sales agreement. Until the pen touches the paper, and actually for a short time afterward, there is no deal.

Until you sign, you can refuse to accept the offer. However, if the offer is for the price and terms for which you listed the property, you could still be liable for a commission to the agent.

It's important to understand, however, that the deal isn't made exactly when you sign. Rather, it's made when the agent or you communicate the fact that you've signed to the buyers. In practice this means that the agent usually calls the buyers and tells them you've accepted and then takes them a copy of the sales agreement signed by you. Technically speaking, the buyers can withdraw the offer any time before they learn of your acceptance, just as you can withdraw a counteroffer anytime before the buyers accept it.

Sometimes you or the buyers are a long distance away. To facilitate the deal, the negotiations may be carried out over the phone. I've agreed to deals from thousands of miles away and then sent a copy of the signed agreement by either express mail or FAX machine. Distances shouldn't keep a deal from happening.

Get a Copy

The agent or the buyers must give you a copy of everything you sign. Be sure that you get that copy and that you hang onto it. Later on, if there should be some dispute over what was actually agreed upon (particularly if counteroffers were scrawled over the original offer), your copy will be your protection. Get it, make sure it contains signatures of the sellers over the last and final counteroffer.

Moving On

Once you've gotten a signed sales agreement, you're halfway home, but not all the way. Now you have to open escrow, deliver clear title, make sure the buyers get their financing, and do those hundred other small things that are necessary before the deal closes.

No, you can't say you've sold your house until the title is recorded and you've gotten your check, but at this stage, you can kick back a bit and relax. Hopefully, the hardest part is over.

10
Perils of Seller Financing

Just a few years ago if someone had asked me about seller financing, I would have suggested that it was an excellent way to facilitate a sale and to get a high interest paying note as well. Today, I'm not so sure. I've seen so many seller-financed deals go sour that I'm beginning to think that perhaps it's something to avoid, if at all possible. Here's why.

What Is Seller Financing?

When you go into the grocery store and buy a jar of mayonnaise, normally you would pay all cash. You'd give the clerk your $1.50 or $2.00 or whatever, take the mayonnaise, and that would be the end of the transaction.

Selling real estate is rarely that simple, particularly in today's high-priced market. Few, very few buyers have cash to pay for the purchase of your home. Rather, they plan to finance most of the purchase price—typically 80 to 90 percent of it.

The usual route for financing is to go to an institutional lender—a bank, a savings and loan, a mortgage banker. This lender gives the buyer the money in exchange for a trust deed (a variation of a mortgage, but more commonly used) on the property. The buyer now gives you the money, which you use to pay off your existing mortgage and your costs of sale as well as taking the remains for yourself, and the deal is made.

However, sometimes the buyers won't or can't go to the institutional lender. Instead, they come to you and say, "Seller, please finance my purchase of your home." As explained in an earlier chapter, they may want you to carry back a second or third mortgage for a portion of the purchase price. If you own your home free and clear, they may *even* want you to carry back a first mortgage.

Seller financing is when you receive "paper" (mortgage or trust deed) instead of cash for your sale. Of course, the real question for you, the seller, is should you do it? Should you finance your property for the buyer?

The Buyers' Motivation

The first thing you should look at when you're considering carrying back paper is the reason the buyers have for asking you to do this. Typically the reasons are all bad, for you. Here are a few reasons buyers want you to carry the financing:

1. The buyers have bad credit and can't get an institutional loan.
2. The buyers can't qualify (don't have enough income) to get an institutional loan for enough money to make the sale.
3. The buyers don't have enough cash for the down payment.
4. Interest rates are so high that the buyers can't qualify for a mortgage.
5. The buyers are investors, and they are looking for a better deal by having you carry the financing.

Your Motivation

Notice that in every case the reason for your carrying paper is to the buyers' advantage. You do it, in other words, not to help yourself, but to help the buyer. Why then, should you bother?

1. You can make a deal that otherwise couldn't be made.
2. You can often get a high-interest paying loan in your favor.

Let's look at the sellers' reasons for carrying financing more closely.

Carrying Financing to Make a Deal

I have a friend, Ann, who has a house in the Dallas, Texas area. Although as of this writing this area of the country is recovering, economically, just a few years ago it was a catastrophe. Falling oil prices caused the housing market to collapse. Very quickly a buyer's market emerged.

Ann, seeing what was happening, tried to get out ahead of the crowd. She put her house on the market as soon as prices started to waver. Even so, there were few buyers.

Ann saw that things were only getting worse and she realized that time was against her, so she told her agent that she was willing to carry all the down payment in the form of paper. A buyer only had to pay the purchaser's portion of the closing costs to move in.

House Sold in Dallas Area

She paid in cash		She received
Her closing costs	$ 4,000	Second mortgage $35,000
Commission	$ 6,000	(her equity)
Total cash	$10,000	

Notice that it cost her $10,000 in cash out of pocket to make the sale. However, since she was getting a second mortgage for $35,000, she felt that she was coming out ahead. The second paid 11 percent interest, which was far more than she could have gotten at the bank at the time.

The economy continued to deteriorate in the area, however, and within six months, the buyers lost their jobs. They decided to move to California. They put the house up for resale; however, they quickly saw that the housing market had gotten so bad that there was little chance to sell soon, if at all. So they simply packed up and left.

The first Ann heard of this was when she didn't receive her monthly second mortgage payment. She waited a week, thinking it had been lost in the mail, then she called the buyers of her house. Their phone was disconnected.

She mailed a letter to the buyers asking for an explanation. The letter was returned—there was no forwarding address. She called the agent who had handled the sale and asked him to investigate. He reported back that the house was locked up and empty. And it looked like quite a mess inside.

He then gave Ann two rather bleak options.

1. She could begin foreclosure proceedings, a fairly swift process in Texas, and take back the property. However, to do this she would have to make up the back payments on the first mortgage (several thousand dollars at that point—the buyers hadn't been paying on the

first) and pay foreclosure costs, another thousand or so. Once she got the house back in her name, it would probably cost her another $3000 to fix it up and put it into good enough shape to make another attempt at reselling.

2. She could simply walk away from the property as the buyers had done and *lose all of her $35,000 second mortgage.*

Ann immediately ruled out option number two. She wasn't going to lose $35,000. She caught a flight to Texas and met with the agent. He showed her the house; it would need repainting and new carpeting throughout—probably at a cost closer to $5000 than $3000. Then the agent pointed out that the market had gone completely cold. Nothing was selling—everything was in foreclosure. If she paid the $10,000 or so it would cost to get the property back and fix it up, she might not be able to sell it for a year or two, if then.

"I'll rent it," was her reply. The agent shook his head sadly. Everyone was trying to rent. Landlords were offering two and three months free rent just to get people to move in.

In the end, Ann realized the futility of it all. She gave up, lost her $35,000, wrote it off to her education in real estate—a very expensive lesson.

The point of Ann's story is that in today's marketplace, if you finance a house in order to make a deal, sometimes you end up with a deal that would have been better not made. In the end you could lose everything.

The reason goes back to the motivations of buyers. Top notch buyers, those who have credit and cash, often don't want seller financing. They want to put down the cash to keep their payments low, and they don't have any problem qualifying for a mortgage.

On the other hand, problem buyers who don't have cash or who can't get new financing, are looking for seller financing. Thus, very often sellers who carry back paper are in reality getting problem buyers, people who can't, or won't, keep up the property or make the payments. These may be people who already have such bad credit that they don't mind walking away if things get rough.

Trap

There's a whole different category of buyers—investors. A spate of "get rich quick in real estate" seminars and books has spawned a group of so-called investors whose whole attitude seems to be, "I can get rich in real estate by taking advantage of sellers." These people often buy property with seller financing, then refinance the property under the seller's loan (we'll see how shortly), take the cash, and leave. The poor seller is stuck in a position even worse than Ann's, for now the property has financing on it, frequently for far more than it's worth.

Carrying Financing for Investment

This is not to say that all seller financing is bad. Sometimes, depending on your motivation for using it, it can turn out quite well.

For example, I have another friend, Chuck. Chuck is about to retire. He has social security, but he's not sure that's enough to live on during retirement. He's looking for another source of income. His biggest asset was the equity in his home, which was all paid off. Chuck's goal was to sell his home, put the money he received in the bank, and live off the interest.

However, at the time, the bank's highest interest was 8 percent. Since Chuck would get about $125,000 from the sale of the home, that meant he would receive roughly $10,000 a year. He had hoped for more.

When it came time to sell, however, the agent suggested that instead of looking for a buyer who would get a new institutional loan, Chuck should carry the first mortgage. Firsts were then paying about 11 percent interest which would translate to about $14,000 a year in income for Chuck. In addition, if he made the loan for 20 or even 30 years, he could be fairly assured of a steady income for a long time to come. Chuck was in the southern California market, which was warm at the time, and the agent felt a sale wouldn't be too hard to make, with or without seller financing.

Chuck thought it was a good idea.

When buyers were found, the agent qualified them just as if they were getting a new institutional loan. They had to have good credit, they had to have sufficient income to "qualify" (roughly three times the monthly payment after all long term debt, such as car payments), and they had to have the normal down payment.

The buyers purchased, and Chuck carried back the financing. It's been nearly six years now and Chuck's monthly check hasn't been late once.

Two Different Outcomes

A large part of the reason behind Chuck's success and Ann's failure has to do with their motivation in carrying back paper. In Ann's case, she felt it was the only way to make a sale. Consequently, she was willing to accept less than desirable buyers.

In Chuck's case, however, the motivation was long-term income. Chuck was only willing to sell to buyers who were totally qualified.

Of course, it must be pointed out that Chuck was selling in a warm market while Ann's market was cold. This, however, only highlights the problem with much seller financing—it is done out of desperation.

Tip

Be aware of your motives when you carry back paper. If you're desperate to sell and using seller financing to attract a buyer, be aware that it might be a less than desirable buyer. You might end up losing more than you gain by making the sale.

How to Use Seller Financing to Your Advantage

Thus far we've looked at examples of what can go wrong and what can go right with seller financing. There are, however, a whole host of variables in between. We'll consider some of these now. At the end of the chapter we'll have a list of items to consider before you offer to finance your buyer.

The Seller Who Outsmarts the Bad Buyer

I know of several sellers who purposely look for unqualified buyers. Their goal is to sell their property to a buyer in the hopes that the buyer will default after a year or more so that they can get the property back through foreclosure. In this way they can keep reselling the same property over and over.

There are two catches to making this plan work. First, the sellers have to keep their costs down. These sellers typically sell FSBO, so they don't have any commission to pay. Their only expenses are the closing costs when they sell and the foreclosure costs later on if they have to take the property back.

Second, they get a large enough down payment from the buyers to cover all their costs plus a profit.

Since it's often a year or more before the buyers default and the sellers foreclose, the market price of the home typically goes up. That means that each time the seller gets the property back, resale can be for a higher price.

I'm not advocating this approach. I'm simply mentioning it to point out that if you want to play the game as a seller, you can play it to win.

The Seller Who Converts Paper into Cash

Paper can be converted to cash, depending on a number of variables. Here's how sellers can take advantage of this conversion.

The sellers have a house to sell which they feel is worth $100,000 on the market in a cash deal. However, they realize it may take a while to find a cash buyer, so they put it up for sale at $105,000 and agree that they'll take partial paper.

Cash sale		Paper sale	
Cash down	$ 20,000	Cash down	$ 10,000
		Second mortgage carried by seller	$ 15,000
New first from bank or S & L	$ 80,000	New first from bank or S & L	$ 80,000
Sales price	$100,000		$105,000

The buyers, presumably, are willing to pay a little more for the house since they don't have to pay all cash down.

Once the sale is made, the seller waits at least six months, during which time the buyer (hopefully) makes regular monthly payments on the $15,000 second mortgage. Then the seller sells that second mortgage to a buyer of seconds for cash—in this case $10,000 cash. The seller ends up with the same $20,000 in cash as would have been received in a cash sale, except that there's a six month delay. However, during that six months the buyer pays a good rate of interest on the money.

The advantage of this sale is that the seller should be able to move the house faster by offering to carry back some of the paper instead of waiting for an all cash buyer.

Why the six-month wait? I'm sure some readers are wondering why the seller waited six months before converting the second to cash. Indeed, the seller could have converted that note to cash in escrow and this is sometimes done. However, buyers of second notes (investors who are looking to make a higher interest on their cash), are wary of "unseasoned" seconds. They don't know if the buyer will actually make the payments or will simply default. Buyers of seconds don't normally want to get involved in foreclosure. An exception is the investor who buys seconds in properties where the owners have huge equities, hoping that those owners will default.

If you sell a second mortgage in escrow, the buyer of that second will normally pay less than if you let it "age" for a minimum of six months. Our seller waited six months to be sure that at least $10,000 cash could be realized from the $15,000 second.

Why only $10,000 for a $15,000 note?   A second question many readers are sure to be asking is why didn't the buyer of the second pay the full $15,000 in cash? Why was there a $5000 discount?

The reason has to do with yield and risk. Yield is the actual percentage rate of interest that a buyer of seconds gets. It is computed in a fairly complex formula that takes into account the interest rate, the amount of cash paid out, and the term of the second. For example, a second mortgage for three years may have a stated interest rate of 12 percent; however, because of the risk of foreclosure in the second mortgage market, an investor may demand a yield of 18 percent. How does the investor get that yield from a 12 percent mortgage?

The answer is by discounting the second mortgage. A 12 percent mortgage which pays $15,000 at maturity, but which only costs the buyer of that mortgage $10,000 in cash, will in fact yield upwards of 18 percent interest. The 18 percent is figured on the $10,000 actually invested.

It's much like zero-coupon government bonds. You pay less than the face value of the bond. The difference is computed as your interest rate over the term.

Thus, by discounting the second mortgage, the seller is able to find an investor who is willing to buy it for cash.

Tip

The trick with offers to carry back a second with the intention of converting it to cash is to get a high enough second. You need to have enough leeway so that when you sell at discount, you get out the cash you need.

What makes a second mortgage saleable?   Finally, it's important to understand that simply taking back a second mortgage as part of seller financing doesn't guarantee you can resell it. Here are the requirements investors are typically looking for in seconds:

1. *High interest rate.* The higher the better.

2. *Three to five year term.* Shorter terms mean that investors have to turn their money around too often. Longer terms mean that the

money is tied up against an uncertain future when interest rate fluctuations could reduce the value of the second.

3. *Late penalty.* This is important. The second should contain a money penalty if the buyers are more than a couple of weeks late in their payment. The reason is simple. If there is no penalty, then each time the buyers are late the holder of the second has only one option—start foreclosure, an expensive proposition. On the other hand, if the second has a penalty, it is easy to enforce and encourages prompt payment.

4. *Proper documents.* Improper documents or documents that are improperly executed account for more failures of seconds than people realize. If you're giving a second as part of the sale, be sure you have a competent attorney check out the documents.

The Seller Who Takes Back a Balloon Payment

Finally, there is an option which helps out the buyer as well as the seller. The seller is aware that the buyers are having trouble qualifying for mortgages. So the seller offers the buyers an "interest only" second mortgage. The buyers will pay, for example, for three years, interest only. After that time the full amount of the mortgage is due. In other words, the sellers get interest for three years, then all of the principle comes due. This is called a balloon payment, when one payment is much higher than the others.

The buyers at the end of the three years normally have to refinance to get enough cash to pay off the balloon second. Many sellers, at the end of the three years, will offer to extend the mortgage for an additional three years at the then current interest rate.

In this way the seller preserves capital all the while receiving a good interest rate on it.

Trap

Beware of mortgage assumptions. In our examples, seller financing consisted of giving the buyers a second mortgage as part of the down payment when they got either a new first, or assumed an FHA or VA (government insured or guaranteed) mortgage. Seller financing, however, *did not involve buyers assuming existing conventional, non-government, first mortgages.*

The reason is simple. In today's marketplace almost no conventional loans are really assumable. When you sell your house, chances are the

buyers cannot take over your existing first mortgage unless it's a VA or
FHA, and then there may be restrictions. If the mortgage does provide
for an "assumption," chances are the buyers have to requalify, pay new
costs, and pay the then current interest rate—which is equivalent to getting a new mortgage.

Checklist for Seller Financing

	YES	NO
1. Are you getting the current market interest rate for seconds?	[ ]	[ ]

Check with agents, the local paper under ads for seconds for sale, and
with mortgage brokers to find the current rate.

	YES	NO
2. Are you giving the right term?	[ ]	[ ]

Seconds over five years are sometimes considered too long-term to be
saleable

	YES	NO
3. Have you checked out the buyers' credit?	[ ]	[ ]

You can get a credit report either directly from a credit agency or
through your agent. If the buyers have any bad credit at all, you're significantly increasing your risk of having to take the property back.

	YES	NO
4. Have you gotten an estimate of foreclosure costs in your state?	[ ]	[ ]

There are professionals who specialize in handling foreclosures. They
often advertise under real estate in the classified section of papers. Or
you can contact an escrow officer or a real estate agent who can direct
you to one. Find out your likely costs now, before you commit.

	YES	NO
5. Are the buyers putting a lot of cash into the property?	[ ]	[ ]

The more cash the buyers put in, the more committed they will be to
holding on to the property and avoiding default. Beware of buyers who
put no cash down.

	YES	NO
6. Are you careful to avoid having a subordination clause in your second?	[ ]	[ ]

A subordination clause makes your second "subordinate" to another mortgage. What this means is that the buyers could refinance the first for more money, making your second virtually worthless. Avoid this like the plague.

	YES	NO
7. Are your documents correct?	[ ]	[ ]

The only way to have any sense of security here is to have them examined by, if not prepared by, a competent real estate attorney.

	YES	NO
8. Have you consulted an attorney and your tax planner/accountant to inform you of the tax consequences of getting a second mortgage?	[ ]	[ ]

In some cases, even though you took back paper, the government may treat the sale as cash and could require you to pay tax on the money that you haven't yet received.

	YES	NO
9. Have you consulted with an expert on seller financing in your area to see if you're handling the deal correctly?	[ ]	[ ]

Each state has somewhat different laws and rules regarding second mortgages. Be sure you're in compliance in your state.

11
Converting a Sale into a Rental

What happens when you have to move to a new area, you've changed jobs for example, and you have to sell your current house in order to be able to afford to buy a new one, yet you can't sell the house?

What happens if you've purchased a new home, contingent upon selling the old one, and you just can't find a buyer for that old one?

What happens if you're looking for an investment house and at the same time decide you need to move from your own house because it's too small, too big, or not close enough to work?

All of the above are not necessarily problems; they could be opportunities in disguise. When you own a home and have to move, selling may not be the correct answer. Converting that home to a rental may prove far wiser, and more profitable, in the long run.

Reasons for Converting to a Rental

There are lots of specific reasons for converting a home you'd rather sell to a rental, but they all boil down to just two:

1. You can't sell because of the current market or because of some other problem with the property.
2. You want the income and equity appreciation that a rental property offers.

I have a friend, Arlie, who owns a house in a suburb of Denver. Arlie was recently transferred to Los Angeles. He put his Denver house up for sale, but the market at the time was cool, and there were no takers. So what did Arlie do?

He didn't give up his new job opportunity. He didn't lose the equity in his house by letting it go to foreclosure. He rented it with the understanding that when the market improved in the Denver area, he would sell it.

As it turned out, prices slowly began to rise in Denver as the price of oil increased, and the market slowly warmed up. While he rented the property, Arlie was able to use it as a write-off on his taxes (there are severe restrictions here, see your accountant), and when he sold, he was able to get a far higher price than he originally had the house listed for. In effect, not selling but renting turned out to be a boon for him.

Problems With Converting a House to a Rental

"But," I'm sure many readers are saying, "I can't do that. I need the money from the sale for the purchase of my new home," or, "I don't know anything about handling rental property," or, "I wouldn't even know where to begin doing such a thing."

Rest assured, there are answers to all of these problems.

1. The Problem of Getting Cash Out in Order to Buy the Next Home

Generally, you can get most of the cash out of your house whether you sell or not. You can get it out by refinancing. It's important, however, that you do this with the proper timing.

For example, let's say that your house is worth $200,000 and you owe $100,000. Your expenses of selling might run $15,000 including commission, so you stand to get $85,000 clear, if you could sell. Your plan is to use that $85,000 as a down payment on your next house.

But, your house just won't sell. The market's bad, the neighborhood isn't terrific, the house could be in better condition, and on and on. The point is that you can't sell it and you certainly don't want to just walk away from all that equity.

You can refinance it. As an *owner-occupant* you are entitled to refinance your home for up to 80 percent of its current value. If you were an investor who owned a rental property, most lenders would only loan you enough to pay off your existing mortgage and closing costs. Being an owner-occupant offers many more opportunities.

If your home is worth $200,000 you should be able to refinance up to $160,000. Less your existing mortgage of $100,000 and roughly $8000 in financing expenses, you could clear about $52,000.

Refinancing

Value	$ 200,000
New first mortgage	$ 160,000
Less existing mortgage	−100,000
Less refinancing expenses	−8,000
Net out	$ 52,000

By refinancing you could net out $52,000. Now that's considerably less than the $85,000 you might hope to net out on a sale, but it's still a fair hunk of cash, and you could certainly use it as a substantial down payment on a second property.

But, you say, you need more. The $52,000 isn't enough. You have two options. You get a home equity loan which may be difficult to find because most institutional lenders will not give a home equity loan when the total indebtedness is in excess of 80 percent of the property value—some, however, will. Or you get a second mortgage for an additional $25,000. Second mortgages are available from mortgage brokers, mortgage bankers, and individuals who advertise for borrowers in the real estate section of your local newspaper.

Two Mortgage Refinancing

From first	$52,000
From second	$25,000
Total net from refinancing	$77,000

Now you're close enough to the $85,000 that you originally wanted to get from the property to make the purchase of that new home.

But, will it work?

Trap

If you apply for the smaller second mortgage first, you may not later be able to get the big first. You should get the refinancing in the order of the mortgages, first then second.

Whether or not you're able to get this refinancing depends to a large degree on your being an owner-occupant. That means that you must secure all your financing *before* you move from your property or even buy another home to move to. In general, once you have the mortgage on your property, lenders don't care whether you continue to occupy it or rent it out. The VA and FHA are exceptions here—in some cases they require you to continue to occupy the property for six months to a year. Some conventional lenders will call the loan if you rent the house—check first.

2. Does It Make Economic Sense?

The next question asked by most people who are considering renting as an alternative to selling is whether or not it makes financial sense.

This is a call you have to make. But there are certain parameters to follow. First, you have to know how much your total payments are going to be after you refinance, and you have to know how much you can rent the property for.

Generally speaking, in order for a rental property to make financial sense, you must be able to cover your mortgage payment, your property taxes, plus your insurance on the property all from the rental. (In the trade that's called PITI—Principle, Interest, Taxes, and Insurance.) That doesn't really mean that you break even, because you still have maintenance, advertising, clean-up, and so forth. But, those expenses are usually manageable, providing the property breaks even on the PITI.

Your first task, therefore, even before you find out about refinancing, is to learn what you can rent your home for. There are many sources for this kind of information:

1. Contact local agents.

2. Look for rentals in your neighborhood and ask the owner what the rental rate is.

3. Check your local paper under "House For Rent—Unfurnished" (unless for some reason you intend to leave your furniture). Look for homes with the same number of bedrooms and baths as yours in similar areas.

4. Check with any rental bureaus in your area.

You may find that you can rent a home in your area for $700 a month or $1000 or $3000, depending on the area and the home. This becomes your base figure.

Now call up a lender and tell that person that you are planning to refinance. Give them a figure for 80 percent of your current house value. Then ask what the monthly mortgage payment would be for the lowest interest rate mortgage available.

Tip

If you're planning to rent out your property for only a short time, look for an Adjustable Rate Mortgage (ARM) with a low "teaser" rate. This rate may be 2 to 3 percentage points below the current rate. Be aware that the teaser rate is just that. Usually within two years the mortgage interest rate rises to the current market rate. But by then, hopefully, you'll be able to sell.

Calculate Your Monthly Payments With the New Financing.   Finally, call up a lender of seconds (if you're going to need one) and find out what the monthly payment would be on a second for the amount you're considering.

Now, you've got both your sets of figures. You should already know what taxes and insurance are running you. Compare the figures:

Comparison of Rental Income vs. Basic Expenses

Basic Expenses		Rental Income
Mortgage(s)	$ _____	
Taxes	$ _____	
Insurance	$ _____	
Total	$ _____	$ _____

If rental income is higher, if both figures are the same, or if they are even just close, you have an excellent chance of financially handling the rental of your property. If expenses are higher, then you may want to reconsider renting.

Tip

Don't fall into the mistaken belief that you won't have any other costs beyond PITI. As noted earlier, there will always be maintenance and fix-up expenses. However, hopefully you'll be able to write-off the property (see your accountant to see if you can) and this will more than make up for these other expenses.

Trap

If it turns out that your PITI expenses are far higher than your rental income, don't decide to, "Damn the torpedoes, full speed ahead!"

When expenses exceed rental income, you move into a negative cash flow situation. That means that each month, just to pay the mortgage, taxes, and insurance, you have to take money out of your own pocket. While this may seem easy to do when looking at it theoretically, it's quite different when you're faced with actually spending those hard earned dollars on a house. You may quickly come to call that property a "bottomless pit." In the trade they have a name for houses like this. They are called, "alligators." They just keep biting at you.

If rental income doesn't justify your expenses, try something else such as a lease-option described in an earlier chapter.

3. Emotionally, Can You Live with a Rental?

I have a friend, Philly, who decided to do just what has been described thus far in this chapter. He found that he couldn't sell his home, so he decided to rent and wait until the market got better before selling.

It made financial sense to rent the property; however, Philly just wasn't the sort who made a good landlord. He managed to rent the property, and the first week after the tenants moved in, they called him at 11 at night to say that the sink in the master bathroom was dripping and they couldn't sleep. Could he please come over and fix it?

Those who rent property on a regular basis would have "sweet talked" the tenants, expressing concern, suggesting they turn the water off underneath the sink, and assuring them that a plumber (or the landlord) would be out first thing in the morning.

Philly, however, had just fallen asleep when the phone rang. When he heard the problem, his response was to shout into the phone that they were disturbing his sleep and that they could damned well fix their own faucet.

At the end of the month, the tenants moved out.

Philly had to rent the place all over again. The next tenants were better. They waited until the second week to call, complaining that their furnace wouldn't go on, it was the middle of winter, and they were cold.

Philly tried to handle it better. He suggested that they build a fire in the fireplace and he'd send out a heating repair person the next day. He did, and it turned out the heat exchanger on the furnace was broken. He needed a new furnace to the tune of $1200.

He exploded. He didn't have the cash available. He told the tenants they'd have to wait until the following month when he got the money to fix the furnace.

They moved out the next day and sued him in small claims court for the half month's rent they said they had coming. He tried to argue with the judge, but when the tenants pointed out that he refused to fix the furnace, he lost.

Philly's problems were not actually financial. They were psychological. He could have borrowed the money to fix the furnace. He never quite understood that owning a rental property is like caring for a delicate flower. It has to be watered and pampered in order for it to prosper. Philly didn't want the bother and the headache, he wanted the rental to take care of itself. Unfortunately, that's not the way rentals work.

If you're like Philly, then you shouldn't rent out your home regardless of whether it makes financial sense or not. In the end you'll lose money and perhaps even ruin your health because you'll be doing something for which you are unsuited.

On the other hand, millions of Americans rent millions of homes out each year without much hassle or much bother. And they eventually receive significant profits for doing this. It all depends on your mental attitude.

How to Handle a Rental

Sydney, a young woman living alone, found herself in the predicament of having to move to a new home, yet wanting to purchase a rental home at the same time. She had heard of the profits to be made in owning real estate (indeed, virtually all of the major fortunes made in this country involve real estate), and she wanted to be a part of it.

So, Sydney decided to rent out her present house instead of selling it. She borrowed against it and used the money as a down payment on another house. Then she was faced with renting out her former home.

Since the house was already in good shape, she didn't have to do any fix-up work. So, she placed an ad in the local paper. It was a short 3-line ad which read:

For Rent
Lovely Garden Home
3 bed, 2 bath, with fireplace,
den, large garage, $850 + deposit

She included her phone number and soon she began receiving calls. She screened the prospective tenants to weed out those who could not afford the house or who had families too large for the property. Then she showed it.

Eventually she got several people who wanted to rent. Sydney picked up some rental application forms from a local real estate agent and had the applicants fill them out. Then she chose the most likely prospect for tenant and got a credit report on the person. The credit report was terrible—this person never seemed to pay bills.

So she picked the next likely candidate and got a credit report on this second prospect. This person had perfect credit, so she rented the property, collecting the first month's rent plus a sizeable cleaning and security deposit.

There have been, of course, maintenance problems, but Sydney either corrected them herself or called in local work people to do the job. In over two years of renting, she has had the same tenants and hasn't had any major problems. The housing market in her area has gotten even stronger with good price appreciation. She figures she has made 20 percent on her money by holding the house for the extra time, and now she plans on selling her property for a handsome profit within the next six months.

All of which is to say that if you're willing to give a little time and energy to your rental, as well as use a bit of common sense, it's not that hard to find and keep good tenants and to make a profit on rental property. If you can't or don't want to sell your present house when you move, converting to a rental makes excellent sense in many circumstances.

For more information on managing a rental house, you might check into *How To Find And Manage Profitable Properties* by this author, McGraw-Hill, 1988.

12

Closing the Deal— Escrow and Extra Costs

The final step in selling your home is the "closing." It is the time when you sign the deed and a few other documents, the buyers deposit their final monies into escrow, the lender funds the new loan, and the property actually trades hands. (You do not receive your check until after escrow closes.) It's also the time when a host of things can go wrong to derail the deal.

The Escrow Process

After you signed a sales agreement, either you or the agent opened an "escrow." This is an independent person or corporation who might be called a stake holder. The escrow does only what you and the buyers tell it to do. It handles your title to the property and the buyers' money, and when everything is in order, actually concludes the sale.

Trap

Today the escrow process is used in most states. However in some states, particularly along the east coast, a more informal process is occasionally used in which a real estate attorney handles all of the tasks normally provided by escrow. While custom suggests that this works, my advice is to use an independent and licensed escrow whenever possible. In most states escrows must be corporations licensed by the state, and they must also carry a minimum capitalization and bonding. This gives you some protection. After all, the process of escrow involves handling all of the funds for your home, sometimes hundreds of thousands of dollars. You want some assurance that the person handling these monies isn't going to take off for Acapulco with them.

What Escrow Does

1. Prepares instructions for you and the buyers.
2. Collects all documents.
3. Prepares necessary documents for signatures.
4. Holds all monies in a trust account.
5. Handles prorations.
6. Disperses monies to the appropriate parties.
7. Sends the deed, trust deed, and other documents out for recording.

What Escrow Does Not Do

1. Does not examine the property.
2. Does not secure financing.
3. Does not solve title problems (although the escrow officer can be very helpful in suggesting ways for you to solve title problems).
4. Does not order inspections (termite or building).
5. Does not give advice.

While it should be apparent from these lists that escrow performs important functions, it also should be clear that there are other important matters that it does not concern itself with. As a seller, many of these become your responsibility.

Tip

In most cases the real estate agent will handle all of your needs during the escrow process—after all, the agent doesn't get paid until escrow closes. However, in some cases agents can be lax, allowing important matters to slip. This can cause frustrating delays and can sometimes result in the loss of the deal.

The best way to avoid such problems is to learn what escrow requires of you for your deal and then stay on top of getting it done. If the agent pulls all the various items together, fine. If not, be sure that you're ready to step in and take over.

Beware of Agent-Owned Escrow Companies

Since you, the seller, usually don't handle real estate transactions on a regular basis, the agent will normally suggest a particular escrow company. The agent's choice may or may not be a wise choice.

One reason is that some real estate brokerage companies own their own escrow companies, or at least own an interest in the company. This means several things, one of which is that the broker is getting part of the fee you pay for escrow. There is really nothing wrong with this, *as long as the agent discloses this fact to you and you agree.* An agent who fails to tell you that she is getting a portion of your escrow fee may be violating her fiduciary responsibility to you when she recommends her own company. This is a breach of ethics and, in some states, may even be illegal. Besides, if the agent owns the escrow, how can you be sure that the recommendation to use it is based on the escrow's good service rather than on the agent's desire for an additional fee?

There's yet another reason to use an independent escrow, one not owned by a real estate company, and that's the matter of control. While the essence of escrow is to be an impartial stake holder between buyers and sellers, there are often times when the escrow has the opportunity to take or not take actions that could affect the outcome of the deal.

Delays and Speed-Ups

For example, there's the matter of time. Let's say you signed a sales agreement that calls for a 60 day escrow. You figure, naturally enough, that within two months the house will be sold and you'll need to be out. So you purchase another house, and at the end of 60 days, you're all packed and ready to make the move. Of course, you're depending on the sale of your house in order to get the money to buy the next one.

Only the deal doesn't close. You call the escrow officer and are told there's a short delay because the buyers' lender hasn't funded yet. It's nothing to worry about.

So you wait. Two weeks later the sellers of the house you bought are screaming at you to close their deal. If you don't close, they'll back out of the deal. But, you can't close on the house you bought until you close on the house you're selling. Frantically you call the escrow officer again.

You are told that the lender the buyers were using had a problem and couldn't fund, so now the buyers are finding a new lender. There's going to be at least another 30 day delay.

Thirty days! You blow your stack and call up your agent. You're between a rock and a hard place. You've got to sell your house right away or you'll lose the new home you're buying.

After a lot of hemming and hawing you finally learn that the real problem is that the buyers for your property can't qualify for a mortgage. They've been desperately scrambling from lender to lender and not one will take them. Your agent, to keep from losing the deal and the commission, has told the escrow officer to stall.

Real Problems

What happens? If the buyer never gets a lender, you don't sell...and you can't buy and move into your new home. Presumably you made the purchase of your new home subject to the sale of the your old, so you're not out any money.

It's a real problem that was caused in part by the escrow officer not informing you of what was really happening. Having been told to stall, the escrow agent simply left out important information when you called. Yes, it's true the lender wasn't funding. Yes, it's true that the lender the buyers were using had a problem. What was left out that you desperately needed to know was that you had unqualified buyers. You could have been told that weeks earlier and could have been saved a lot of frustration and problems. In addition, you might have been able to take corrective steps such as putting your house back on the market.

This is certainly not to say that all agent-owned escrows operate this way, but I have seen it happen. While the escrow officer is never "on your side," you don't want that person to be on somebody else's side either.

Trap

Some real estate agents have you sign as part of your listing that you agree to use their escrow company. If you don't sign, they say they won't take the listing. Call this bluff. I've never seen an agent not take a listing for a saleable property because you want to use an independent escrow.

Other times agents will insist that you agree to their escrow company as part of the sales agreement. When you sign to sell the property you also sign to use their escrow. Refuse to sign. An agent cannot make the sale of a home contingent upon using a particular escrow company. A buyer can, or you as a seller can, but an agent cannot. Report an agent who tries this to the state real estate regulatory agency.

Tip

Very likely there will be at least two agents involved in the sale of your home, your seller's agent and a buyers' agent. When you are presented with a sales agreement, you may find a contingency clause written in that says you agree to use an escrow company named by the buyers' agent, which may be a company owned by that agent.

In this circumstance, chances are the buyers' agent suggested that the buyers use the company, and the buyers, unwittingly, agreed. If you now sign the agreement with this contingency in it, you are bound to use that escrow company.

My suggestion is that whatever else you do with the offer, you consider crossing out that contingency. Yes, you do risk losing the deal. However, I can't ever recall seeing a deal fall through solely over a disagreement over an escrow company.

Choosing Your Escrow Company

Ideally you should ask your agent to recommend two or three different escrow companies. Then you would choose. If you don't have an agent, you'll find escrow companies listed in the yellow pages of your phone book under either Real Estate Escrow or Real Estate Title Insurance.

In most cases escrow companies work together with title insurance companies so that you can kill two birds with one stone by selecting both the escrow and the title insurance company at the same time.

What To Look For When Selecting An Escrow Company

1. Fees—In many cases the seller pays either all or half of the escrow and the title insurance fees. Comparison shop for fees of different companies.

2. Recommendations—Ask the escrow officer for recommendations. Normally an escrow company goes through hundreds of deals a year. Surely there must one or two buyers or sellers who could recommend their services.

3. Location—All else being equal, get an escrow company that's located close to home. It'll save you long trips when bringing in documents.

4. Size—While getting a large escrow company is not a guarantee of good service, it does usually mean that there's sufficient staff to fulfill any needs that you have.

The Escrow Steps

The procedure that escrow uses can sometimes be confusing. If you understand it going in you have a lot better chance of avoiding frustration and problems.

Step One—Escrow Instructions

To open an escrow, you would normally bring in the sales agreement. The escrow officer would examine the sales agreement and then prepare two sets of instructions based on that agreement, the buyers' and the sellers' sets. Essentially both sets are the same, although buyers and sellers may have different requirements.

The escrow instructions (also called "preliminary escrow instructions") are not directions for you. They are instructions for the escrow company telling it what to do in order to complete the deal. For example, the instructions might state that the buyer is to put in so much cash, get so much money from a new mortgage, and pay for certain fees. They would also state that you the seller are to provide clear title, pay off the existing mortgage, and pay for certain fees such as a termite clearance.

Read the escrow instructions carefully.

Think of them as a kind of second and perhaps more binding sales agreement. You'll be held to whatever's in them. Pay particular attention to:

1. Deposit—Is it to be given to escrow? What happens to it if the buyers renege? (If it's not spelled out in the instructions it could remain in limbo in escrow indefinitely.)

2. Down payment—When is it to be deposited to escrow? Is it to be in the form of cash?

3. Financing—Is it spelled out exactly as you agreed in the sales agreement?

4. Payoffs—Are your loan payoffs stipulated?

5. Prorations—Is the date for prorating correct? (Discussed shortly.)

6. Costs—Are there any unusual or excessive costs that you have to pay?

7. Understanding—Do you fully understand and agree with the escrow instructions? If not, get an explanation and, if necessary, the advice of an attorney.

Step Two—Discovering Title Problems

The second step is different for buyers and sellers. At this juncture the buyers normally go out and seek new financing. You, however, are going to have to clear the title to your property. "No problem," you say. Maybe.

Title problems crop up from the darndest places. Maybe you had a rug cleaning a couple of years ago and the cleaner did a terrible job. You refused to pay, and the cleaner finally said, okay, don't worry about it. But now, when you go to sell, you find that the cleaner put a mechanic's lien on your property for the amount of the cleaning plus costs and interest. The title company won't give clear title until the lien is removed.

Or, fifteen years ago you were in an auto accident. It wasn't a big deal and the other person was at fault. The insurance companies paid off and you promptly forgot about it. However, unbeknownst to you, the other party went to small claims court and secured a judgement against you. That judgement was filed against your property. The title company won't give clear title until that judgement is cleared.

(How can a small claims judgement be filed against you if you didn't know there were court proceedings? In some areas of the country notice of the proceedings, which must be served to you, used to be delivered via "sewer service"…dumped in the garbage. If you didn't show up the other person automatically won. It doesn't happen often today, but if the judgement was way back when, it could have happened.)

Or when you bought the property you needed a co-signor on the mortgage in order to qualify. You had old Uncle Charley sign. Now Uncle Charley's name is on the title to the property, only Uncle Charley died two years ago. The title company won't give clear title until Uncle Charley signs off.

These and other problems, such as a neighbor's suit over an overreaching fruit tree, broken fences, a zoning or building department problem with the city, or any of a dozen other items could crop up. This is not to say that they will, but they could. Normally, the title company will inform the escrow officer of the problem and that officer will inform you and your agent. Now it's up to you to straighten things out.

Clearing Title Problems. Sometimes clearing the title problem is simple. You just pay off the mechanic's lien or the judgement. But, you say, you shouldn't have to because you don't owe the money. True, you can take it to court, spend months or even years battling, and perhaps lose the sale of your home along the way. Or you can call the lien holder or judgement holder and demand they sign off the lien, or you can offer to pay a quarter or half if they'll sign off. Or you can just pay.

Trap

In the past there were unscrupulous individuals who would place liens on properties on which they were owed nothing, usually for small amounts, a few hundred dollars. Placing a lien or other encumbrance, particularly in the form of a mortgage or trust deed, was easy. A person just went down to the county recorder's office and recorded it. In those days many counties required the notarization of only one name on the document for recording.

When a home owner went to sell, the lien was discussed. Since it was only a few hundred dollars, the owner usually found it easier to pay than to argue.

Today this practice has generally stopped because of the penalties against it and because many county recorders now require the notarization of all signatures to a document. However, if you've owned your house for a long period of time, you may find one of these "clouds" on your title. Your best bet, if you do, is to have your agent confront the lien holder and demand its removal, otherwise you'll need to go to the district attorney with a complaint.

Some title problems, however, don't involve money. Uncle Charley's dead, so it's going to be pretty tough to get his signature releasing his interest in the property. But, you can go to the administrator or executor of his estate, if there is one, and get a sign-off, usually with court approval. Or you may have to contact heirs or even go to court. Hopefully, it will be a simple process, but sometimes it isn't.

The city or county may have put a hold on your property because you're not in compliance with some ordinance such as setback or building an addition without a permit. They probably could force you to make corrections, but some local governments prefer just to put a hold on the title. They won't let you sell until you bring the problem in compliance. There's not much you can do, in this case, but comply.

Step Three—Get All Inspections

In addition to clearing title, you must also get all necessary inspections. If you haven't already done so, that includes a house inspection, as described in an earlier chapter, and a termite inspection. Normally the escrow won't order these for you. Rather, you have to contact the various companies and get the required clearances sent to escrow. Agents will often do some of this for you.

Step Four—Sign Off

Normally you're not asked to sign off, that is, to sign the deed officially transmitting the property to the buyers, until escrow is ready to close. Escrow is ready to close when all the conditions setting it up have been met. These include your supplying clear title, getting inspections, and taking care of any other details, and the buyers providing the cash down payment and funding from a lender.

Normally to sign off you'll need to go down to the escrow company and sign before the escrow officer. You'll be asked to sign a deed and a few other documents including a final escrow instructions sheet. This final sheet will show a complete breakdown of the monies from the deal and most importantly, what you'll get. We'll cover your costs shortly.

Tip

In the past agents would often take escrow instructions out of the escrow office and bring them to your home where you could sign. If the agent was a notary public, the document could be notarized there, saving you time.

In recent years, however, irregularities in notarized documents have suggested that sometimes those documents taken out of the escrow officer, weren't always signed by the people whose signature appeared on them. As a result, many escrow companies today require both buyers and sellers to come in and sign. Many lenders also make this a requirement as part of getting the new mortgage.

Once you sign, you just go home and wait. Presumably the buyers are signing their final instructions, the new mortgage, and their other papers. Once escrow is complete, the escrow officer simultaneously records your deed to the buyers, the lenders mortgage, and any other required documents. As soon as everything is recorded, a check can be issued to you.

Avoiding Extra Costs

Unfortunately, most of the costs that you will get as part of the closing of your transaction are going to be pretty much fixed well in advance.

There won't be a great deal you can do about them. What you can watch out for is that you're not paying some of the buyer's costs or that you're not paying for some things that just weren't done. Here's a checklist of typical seller's closing costs:

Checklist of Closing Costs

	YES	NO
1. Commission	[ ]	[ ]

If you've used a real estate agent and signed a listing, you can well expect to pay a commission. Just check to be sure that it's correct. Normally it's based on a percentage of the sales price. It takes only a moment to calculate.

	YES	NO
2. Taxes	[ ]	[ ]

Normally you're required to pay your portion of taxes until the date of proration (explained below). Be sure the proration date is correct as is the sum you're being asked to pay. If you pay your taxes in advance, as can be done in most areas, you may be receiving money back here.

	YES	NO
3. Insurance	[ ]	[ ]

The buyers may be taking over your fire and homeowner's insurance policy. If they are, be sure that they're paying you for the unused portion. You often get money back here too.

	YES	NO
4. Liens and assessments	[ ]	[ ]

As discussed earlier, you're normally expected to pay these off before title can clear. Be sure you understand any that are in effect and that the dollar amounts are correct.

	YES	NO
5. Title insurance/escrow charges	[ ]	[ ]

You should have been told in advance what portion of these, if any, you need to pay. Normally it's done by custom in your area. For example, the sellers may pay escrow while the buyers pay title insurance or both parties may split both costs. Be sure you're not being charged an excessive amount.

Trap

Sometimes buyers will write in a contingency in the sales agreement that the sellers must pay for title insurance and escrow fees. If you signed such an agreement, you'll probably have to pay to close the deal. The time to argue about it is before you sign the sales agreement, not when you're ready to close escrow.

	YES	NO
6. Inspection and other fees	[ ]	[ ]

There are all kinds of inspection and other fees that can be assessed to you. These include:

	YES	NO
Termite inspection fee	[ ]	[ ]
Termite removal costs	[ ]	[ ]
Recording deed costs	[ ]	[ ]
Assumption fees (if buyers assumed your loan)	[ ]	[ ]
Home warranty cost	[ ]	[ ]
Tax service contract (if you're giving a second mortgage)	[ ]	[ ]
Attorney's fees	[ ]	[ ]
Document preparation fees	[ ]	[ ]
Mailing costs (if any)	[ ]	[ ]
Other fees and costs	[ ]	[ ]

The question you need to ask yourself, of course, is whether these costs are necessary and reasonable or not. Ask yourself if the cost came as a surprise or seems excessive.

You should know in advance what the cost for a termite inspection is. You should have agreed to the costs for removing the termites. Similarly, you should have agreed to a home warranty cost and should know what it is. And if you've used an attorney, you should have discussed fees well in advance.

Most of the other costs should be minor. You shouldn't have more than $50 in recording fees. A tax service contract lets you know if the buyers don't pay their taxes and is used when you give them a second or other mortgage. The cost is usually under $25. Assumption fees, mailing costs, and other incidental fees should be very small as well.

Trap

Be wary of "document preparation fees." This is a definite no-no. The escrow officer is being paid to prepare the documents. You shouldn't have to pay extra for that.

What to Do If Final Instructions (or Costs) Are Wrong

You've been told that escrow is ready to close and you need to go into the escrow office and sign the documents. You arrive, and a pile of documents is placed before you. You begin looking over the list of costs and see that instead of a 6 percent commission, you're being charged 7 percent. Or you're being charged for all the escrow and title insurance costs instead of splitting them with the buyer. Or the arithmetic on the prorations doesn't make sense.

What should you do?

If it happened to me, I wouldn't sign. As soon as you sign the documents, you agree to them, errors and all. That doesn't mean that they can't be straightened out later, but it's more difficult once you've signed.

If there's a problem with the commission, it should be a simple matter to solve. Go back to the sales agreement. It should state exactly what the commission is.

Tip

I once was witness to a deal where the sellers signed a listing for a 5 percent commission; however, the agent put in 6 percent on the sales agreement. The sellers didn't pay any attention to the commission amount on the sales agreement and didn't discover the problem until escrow was ready to close.

When confronted, the agent maintained that the sellers had agreed to the higher rate. The sellers were aghast and refused to sign. Further, they threatened to report the agent to the state licensing agency. The agent relented and took 5 percent.

The moral of this story is: read and pay attention to everything you sign. Remember, your signature usually protects the other person, not you.

If the fees have been improperly assessed, go back to the sales agreement. That is the document on which escrow is based. Ask the escrow officer to correct them.

The escrow officer is sure to protest, since correcting means redrawing the documents for buyer and seller. On the other hand, it's not the escrow officer's money, it's yours.

If there's a mistake in math, point it out. The escrow officer should correct it on the spot.

Do You Need an Attorney at Closing

The answer is maybe. If there's a problem, you may need one. If there's no problem, then you probably don't. It's always a good idea to have an attorney check over any documents before you sign, and real estate attorneys often will work for you throughout a transaction for a set fee, often under $500.

Prorations

Prorations are simple to understand, as long as you don't worry over them too much. There are some costs, such as taxes and insurance, which are ongoing. When a house is sold, you the seller should pay your share up until the time the title transfers, then it should be the buyer's responsibility. "Prorating" simply means determining which portion of the costs is the buyers' and which portion is the sellers'.

In order to prorate, a date must be set upon which the prorations are based. Typically this is the close of escrow, although any other date can be used. Since you as a seller may pay taxes and insurance in advance, you can sometimes expect to get money back from prorations.

Trap

Beware of any sales agreement that writes in a specific date for prorations instead of saying, "close of escrow." If the deal closes early, you could end up paying a portion of the buyers' fair share of costs.

13

Deferring Taxes on the Sale of Your Home

In 1986 the federal government passed a tax reform bill which did away with capital gains. This was a real blow to those who intended selling investment real estate. However, at the same time, Congress kept what is probably the most generous tax advantage available to Americans—the residence deferral.

Residence deferral allows you to put off paying taxes on the gain you make when you sell your home for a profit. In other words, if you meet all the requirements you can move from one residence to another and put off the payment of taxes on your profits.

Note: Over the past decade the government has either changed the tax law or its interpretation of that law on virtually an annual basis. In addition, the tax laws as they relate to real estate have become increasingly complex. For those reasons it is suggested that the reader use the following information as an overview of deferral and other tax procedures and leave the determination of the tax consequences of selling any specific property to a competent accountant or tax attorney.

Trap

It's important to understand that the deferral rule does not mean that you get out of paying taxes or that they are forgiven. You still owe the full amount. You are, however, allowed to push the time for payment of that amount into the future. As long as you continue to own your own home and meet the requirments, you do not have to pay the taxes. It's

143

sort of like pushing a snowball uphill. It keeps getting bigger and heavier, but as long as you keep pushing, it never bowls you over.

The deferral rule often prompts people to ask whether or not they will ever have to pay taxes. Can they be deferred forever?

The answer is, maybe. The taxes don't come due as long as you own your own home and meet the requirements. Eventually, if you do sell out at some time in the future, there is a "once in a lifetime $125,000 exclusion" which may be available to you and which may offset most of the gain. (See the next chapter.) On the other hand, if you own your home until you die, your heirs have to worry about your estate, and since they may take over your home at a new tax base, even they may not have to pay. Estate taxation is a complex subject—see your accountant or tax attorney.

How Deferral Works

Essentially deferral is quite easy. When you sell your house for more than you paid, you generally have gain (explained shortly). Normally under today's tax structure, you would add that gain to your other income for the year and pay taxes on it. For example, if your gain were $20,000, you'd add that money to your income and, depending on your tax bracket, pay federal plus state taxes on the total. The taxes, obviously, would eat a lot of your gain.

With deferral, however, you can take that gain and apply it to your next house, if you meet the rules. Instead of paying taxes immediately, they are deferred into the future. You don't have to add that $20,000 to your income. You don't have to pay taxes on it in the year you sold your house.

When you sell your next house, you may be able to again defer the taxes to yet another house. There is no limit to the number of times you can defer your gain. You can, thus, keep rolling over that gain, increasing it with each home you sell, and in effect, end up never paying taxes on it.

Does it really work? Millions of Americans who are doing it suggest that it works very well indeed.

Deferral Rules

Here are the rules that govern tax deferral. Please note that tax rules change constantly as do their interpretation. Before taking any action that would have tax consequences, be sure you contact your accountant or tax attorney.

1. You have two years to roll over your gains

This rule means that from the time you sell your current house, you have two years before or after, a total of 48 months in which to purchase and move into your next home, if you want to defer the gain. If you wait too long, you could lose the deferral advantage. Generally speaking, the rule requires that you physically occupy your new property.

Tip

The two-year rule means not only two years *after* you sell your present home but also two years *before* you sell it. For example, you could buy your next home, move in, and then put your present home up for sale. It might take you 18 months to sell it. The deferral rule applies since the sale and occupancy of your new home came within the two year period.

The rules also apply to the building of a new home. You could sell your present home and live in an apartment for 18 months while your next house is being built. As long as your next house is completed and you are able to move in before two years have elapsed since the sale of your previous house, you can defer gain.

2. Deferral only applies to your personal residence

This is a mistake that many people make. They erroneously believe that they can roll over a rental or a vacation house that they own because it is residential property.

The key is not whether it's a house, a condo, a four-plex, a townhouse, a vacation house, or some other kind of residential property. The key is that it must be your *principal residence*.

You can only have one principal residence at a time. If you have two houses, one a vacation home, the other a home in the city, only one can be your principal residence...on only one can the tax on gain be deferred.

Tip

___

The rules for what constitutes your principle residence can be quite liberal. It can be a single-family house, one-half of a duplex, one-fourth of a four-plex, a condo or timeshare, or some other form of property. You might even maintain that a boat on which you lived and which was permanently anchored in a harbor was your principal residence. (See your accountant.)

Trap

___

If you have two homes, one a vacation home and the other a town home, and sell both simultaneously, generally speaking the one which you occupied for the longest period may be construed as your principal residence, even if its not the house you're currently living in. For example, you live in a house in the city for five years. Then you buy and move into a house in the country in which you live for six months. Next, you sell both properties. You might think that the country house was your principal residence since you occupied it most recently. The government, however, would likely insist that your city house was your principal residence since you occupied it the longest time before the sale of both properties.

If part of your principal residence is investment property, only that part in which you live can be deferred. For example, if you own a duplex and rent out one half, only the half in which you live is considered your principal residence. When you sell, half your gain can be deferred, the other half is taxed in the year of the sale.

This gets even trickier if you use an office in your home. If one-seventh of your home is used as an office (and you take a deduction for it on your taxes), then when you sell your home, six-sevenths of the gain can be deferred, but you'll have to pay tax on one-seventh of the gain.

3. There is a two-year wait between deferrals

At one time people were buying and selling their homes on a rapid basis, rolling over the gain. More recently, however, the government has begun imposing a two-year wait. What this means is that you can use the deferral rule only once every two years.

For example, you sell your principal residence and buy a second house, deferring your gain on the sale. Within 12 months you sell that second house, purchase a third, and make a second gain. You cannot defer the gain on the middle property. However, if you wait two years between the time you sold your first house and the time you sell your third, you can defer the gain on the third.

4. The deferral is based on the price of the new home

In order to get the full deferral you must buy a new home that costs more than your old one. For example, if you sell a house for $100,000 and buy a new house for $101,000, all the gain on the sale of the old house can be deferred.

Trap

This is a very tricky concept and has led some people to think that the *only* way you can get the deferral is to buy a more expensive home than the one you sold. This is the only way you can get the *full* deferral. You can, however, get a partial deferral even if the new house you buy costs less than the house you sold.

For example, you sell a house for $100,000 and buy another for $90,000. The new house costs $10,000 less. This means that you'll pay tax in the year of the sale on the first $10,000 of gain from your first house—it cannot be deferred. But any additional gain, can.

Tip

You can increase the price of the home you purchase even *after* you move in provided you make the improvement within the two-year time limit. For example, you purchase a second home 12 months after the sale of your first home. The new home costs $110,000, the old home sold for $120,000. The new home costs $10,000 less than the old home sold for. Presumably this $10,000 cannot be deferred.

However, within the next six months you add on an extra bedroom to the new home at a cost of $10,000. This addition boosts the basis for the new home to $120,000, meaning that all of the gain from the sale of your old property can be deferred.

Understanding What Taxable Gain Means

It's important to understand that the deferral rule refers to *gain* on the sale of your principal residence. Those unfamiliar with taxation methods, however, are often confused by "gain." It all has to do with your tax basis.

The initial tax basis of your home is established when you purchase it. Your basis is your cost, plus some expenses of purchase, plus any improvements.

Tax Basis

Purchase price	$110,000
Plus costs of purchase	+ 7,000
Plus improvements	+ 5,000
Adjusted basis	$122,000

Trap

Don't forget to add improvements to your home when calculating your adjusted basis. If you add a room or a pool, for example, it should be included.

Also, be aware that not all costs of purchase can be added to your purchase price for the purpose of calculating your basis. Generally speaking those costs which are maintenance as well as those which are deductible in the year of purchase cannot be added to the purchase price when calculating basis. These include, for example, insurance premiums, tax prorations and some points.

Once you've calculated your tax basis, you can determine the gain on the sale of your home. Let's say, for example, that your adjusted basis is $108,000. Now you sell your home for $150,000. You must now calculate your adjusted sales price which is what you sold your home for, less your basis, to get to your gain.

Adjusted Sales Price

Sales price	$150,000
Less costs of sale	$ 10,000
Adjusted sales price	$140,000

Tip

The sales costs which you can deduct from the sales price when calculating your adjusted sales price include such things as commission, title insurance, and escrow costs. Generally speaking they do not include such things as prorated taxes. (Property taxes can be deducted in the year of purchase.) You may also deduct some costs of fixing up the property if they relate directly to the sale. (See discussion later in this chapter.)

Once you've determined both your adjusted basis and your adjusted sales price, it's a simple matter to calculate your gain on the sale.

Gain on Sale

Adjusted sales price	$ 140,000
Adjusted basis	− 108,000
Gain	$ 32,000

This $32,000 is what you would normally pay tax on. Figuring a federal income tax rate of roughly 30 percent, it means that the tax you would owe would be about $10,600. If, however, you use the deferral rules, you can roll over all of this gain and end up not paying any taxes on the sale in the year that it occurred.

Calculating the Basis on Your New Home

Once you know the gain on the sale of your old home, you can calculate the new basis on the next home that you purchase using the deferral rules. Let's say that you purchase your new home for $200,000, substantially more than what you sold your old one for. This means that all of the gain is deferred. Your adjusted price might look like this:

Adjusted Price of Next Home

Purchase price	$200,000
Costs of purchase	$ −5,000
Adjusted purchase price	$195,000

If this were the first house that you had purchased, then the $195,000 figure would be your new basis. However, since you have deferred gain from the sale of your old home, you must now use it to lower your basis.

Calculating Adjusted Basis on Next Home

Adjusted purchase price	$ 195,000
Deferred gain	$ −32,000
Adjusted basis of next home	$ 163,000

Note that the effect of rolling over the deferred gain is to lower the basis for your next home. This effectively carries forward the gain. When you sell your next home you can either carry forward that gain again, or if you do not defer it, pay tax on it at that time.

Tip

If you have trouble seeing how this works, consider this. The next home you buy has an adjusted purchase price of $195,000. Let's say that you are able to sell it for just that amount, an adjusted sales price of exactly $195,000. In other words, you don't make a penny on it. You are still, however, liable for a $32,000 gain because your adjusted basis in the property has been lowered to $163,000. ($195,000 minus $163,000 = $32,000.) Remember, deferring gain simply means pushing it off onto the next property and into the future. It doesn't mean that it's forgotten, forgiven, or overlooked.

Trap

Don't think that just because you've deferred once, you have to pay taxes the next time. As long as you follow the rules (only one sale every two years, stay within the other time limits, etc.), you can keep on doing this as long as you live. You can continue to defer indefinitely.

It's important to understand that you cannot choose to pay taxes on your gain in the year it occurs. The deferral is not optional. If you replace your old principal residence with a new one within the time limits, you must defer the gain.

The Difference Between Gain and Profit

The real confusion over gain comes from a tendency to think that gain means profit. Profit has a much different meaning to most of us. For example, let's say that we purchase a house for $110,000 with a $90,000 mortgage on it. We own it for a few years, and it goes up in value. We decide to take some of that equity out, so we refinance and get a new first mortgage for $120,000.

A few years later we need some more money, so we take out a second mortgage for another $10,000. Now we owe $130,000 on the property.

Finally, it's time to sell and we sell for $150,000. Our costs of sale are $10,000. What's our profit?

Figuring Profit on Sale

Sales price	$ 150,000
Less costs of sale	$ -10,000
Adjusted sales price	$ 140,000
Less mortgages	$ 130,000
Profit	$ 10,000

For most of us, profit means the cash we get when we sell the property. In this case, the cash is $10,000. However, since this is the exact same example as we used for figuring gain, we should quickly see that the gain is substantially different.

Comparing Gain on Sale

Adjusted sales price	$ 140,000
Adjusted basis	-108,000
Gain	$ 32,000

The gain on the sale is $32,000 while the profit is $10,000. Since the gain is what we pay taxes on, it's the more important figure.

Tip

The reason for the discrepancy is that gain is calculated on a cash basis, without regard to financing on the property. Most home owners, however, calculate profit by subtracting the mortgages from the sales price.

Remember in our example, that the owner refinanced twice, taking out cash each time. It's not just the cash that you get when you sell that counts, but also the cash you took out while you owned the property.

Fixing-Up Costs

Since any costs of sale reduce your adjusted sales price (and hence your gain), it's to your advantage to account for all allowable costs of sale. These include reasonable expenses that you incurred in fixing up your home for sale.

Fix-up costs refer to painting, wall papering, carpet cleaning, and so forth. They include both the cost of materials and the cost of labor.

Fix-up costs, however, do not account for a capital expense such as putting on a new roof or adding a new room. These, however, may be used to increase your adjusted basis in the property as discussed earlier—they fall in the realm of improvements.

Sometimes the distinction between fix-up and capital improvments is a close call. For example, if you recarpet the home in order to make a sale, is that a fix-up cost or a capital improvement?

There are also time limits with regard to fixing up a property. If you intend to use fix-up costs to change your basis, check with an accountant first.

Reporting the Sale of Your Home

You should report the sale of your home in the year the sale occured on form 2119, Sale of Your Home. *If you have any taxable gain you should report it on Schedule D, Capital Gains and Losses.*

The question arises sometimes over whether you must pay tax on the gain if you intend to buy a new home within the two-year period, but haven't yet done so.

Generally speaking, if you haven't yet bought a second home, you can choose to either pay taxes on the gain in the current tax year or to defer the payment of taxes. Each course, however, has consequences.

1. If you choose to defer paying taxes on a gain and then later on do not buy a second home before the time period runs out, you must go back and amend your tax return in the year of the sale and pay the taxes as well as interest on the taxes.

2. If you pay taxes in the year of the sale and later buy a second home within the two year period, you can go back and amend your tax return and receive back as a refund the taxes that you paid.

Remember, you cannot choose not to defer paying taxes on the gain if you roll over your principal residence within the appropriate time limits.

Calculating Gain If a Portion of Your Principal Residence Was Investment Property

Many people use a portion of their home as an office. Some rent out a portion of their home—for example, if you own a duplex. When a part of your home is your personal residence and a part is business property, the whole matter of roll over becomes more complex.

The general rule is that you can defer tax only on the gain from that portion of your home which was exclusively your personal residence. You cannot defer paying tax on a gain from that portion which was business or investment property. Thus the tax on that portion of the gain attributable to your personal residence can be deferred. The tax on that portion of the gain attributable to your business, on the other hand, must be paid in the year you sell the house.

While this is straightforward on the surface, the complexity comes from the different methods of calculating basis for investment versus personal property. With investment property, frequently there is the added factor of depreciation which is not a consideration with your principal residence.

Depreciation acts to lower the tax basis on that portion of the property which has a business use. For example, one-tenth of your home may be an office which is depreciated. That depreciation lowers the basis on that one-tenth. When you sell, the amount you lowered the basis through depreciation is added to the gain. Perhaps an example will help to explain.

Calculating Depreciation for a Home-Office

Value of property (building not land—land cannot be depreciated)	$60,000
Term of depreciation—27.5 years[*]	÷ 27.5
Amount to be depreciated in current year	2,182
1/10th office usage	× .10
	$ 218

[*]The term of depreciation for residential real estate has been changed fairly frequently by new tax bills. As of this writing it is 27.5 years, calculated on a straight-line (no acceleration) basis.

In the current year the depreciation for the office portion of the home would be $218. This is the amount you would write off on your income taxes.

However, when you sold, this is the amount by which the basis of your home would be lowered. In other words, the $218 would come back at you as gain upon sale.

Further, when you sell, if one-tenth of the home was used as an office, one-tenth of the gain attributable to the sale would not be deferrable. If your gain on the sale was, for example, $50,000, you could roll over nine-tenths of that or $45,000, but you would have to pay tax in the year of sale on the one-tenth of the gain, $5000, that was attributable to your business use.

Tip

Qualifying for an office in a home means that you must meet stringent requirements, the toughest of which are that the space for the office must be used exclusively and regularly for business purposes. If you use the space to store personal items or have a TV in it where the kids watch shows, you probably can't claim it as personal use. (Check into government publication 587, Business Use Of Your Home.)

Because of the strict qualifying requirements, and because of the hassle it causes upon sale of your home, many people who have a legitimate office at home do not claim it. (Note: if the office in your home is your sole place of business, you may be required to claim it as such.)

14
The $125,000, Once-in-a-Lifetime Exclusion

There's a catch to deferral. In the last chapter we talked about deferring the gain on the sale of your principal residence indefinitely. Every two years or more you could sell your old residence and buy a new principal residence, and as long as you met the requirements of the deferral rule, you could legally avoid paying taxes.

The trouble is that when many of us reach retirement age, we need to cash in the house. It may be our largest single source of wealth. There may be $100,000 or more tied up in the property, and that money is needed to live on.

Retirees

A great many retirees will sell their homes and either buy a much less expensive condo or a mobile home or even move into an apartment. Upon retirement they just don't need a big house. They need a smaller place and the money that's in equity in the property.

The trouble is that when the house is sold, all that gain that had been deferred, perhaps from multiple sales, comes back. Remember, unless you buy a *more expensive home*, you must pay tax on at least a portion of the gain from the sale.

All at once taxes have to be paid on what could be virtually all of a retiree's equity, perhaps more. At a federal tax rate of 27 percent (or more) plus state taxes, that could wipe out close to 40 percent of retirement capital.

The result of this problem was that many retirees were forced to keep a big house that they didn't want and couldn't afford.

Note: Over the past decade the government has either changed the tax law or its interpretation of that law on virtually an annual basis. In addition, the tax laws as they relate to real estate have become increasingly complex. For those reasons it is suggested that the reader use the following information as an overview of deferral and other tax procedures and leave the determination of the tax consequences of selling any specific property to a competent accountant or tax attorney.

The $125,000 Exclusion

To help overcome this problem, in 1980 the government passed a special $100,000 exclusion, which was raised to $125,000 in 1981. The current $125,000 exclusion allows you to escape taxes up to that amount when you sell your home.

What this means is that when you retire and sell your principal residence (moving to a less expensive home or even renting), up to $125,000 of the gain you had been deferring for all those years is excluded—you don't have to pay taxes on it. (Note: It's up to $125,000 of the gain that's excluded, not $125,000 worth of taxes.) Here's an example:

Using the Exclusion

Sales price of your current home	$ 200,000
Basis of your current home	−50,000
Taxable gain	$ 150,000
Sales price of your current home	$ 200,000
The exclusion	−125,000
Adjusted sales price	$ 75,000
Basis	$ 50,000
Taxable gain	$ 25,000

Notice that in this example, without the exclusion, you'd have to pay taxes on $150,000 worth of gain. With it you only have to pay taxes on $25,000.

Of course, you have to meet certain requirements; however, those requirements are not difficult, and for most Americans who own their own principal residence, this ruling has been a godsend. To see if you can qualify for it, read the material that follows and check with your accountant or tax advisor.

Exclusion Rules

While the exclusion rules seem simple enough on the surface, closer examination often raises some questions. Here are the rules and answers to common questions regarding them:

You must be 55 years of age on the day the sale closes (title changes hands).

Question: What if we're married, but only one of us is 55 on the date of the sale and the other is younger?

Answer: You both qualify. Only one spouse has to be 55 on the date of the sale for both to qualify. You must, however, claim it jointly.

Tip

You are considered to be 55 one day before your 55th birthday. Thus, if you turned 55 one day after your house was sold, you would still qualify.

You may only claim the exclusion once in your lifetime.

Question: What if I claimed it once before, but now I've remarried and my wife has never claimed it? Can she claim it now?

Answer: The answer is no. If you and your wife own the home as community property (or tenants in common or tenants by entirety), you must both join in the choice to exclude. Since you've already excluded once before, you are barred from excluding again.

Question: Can a single person claim the exclusion?

Answer: Certainly. In addition you get the full exclusion, $125,000, not just half as is the case in other exclusions. Note, however, that if you marry and your spouse has not claimed it before, he or she cannot claim it again as noted above.

The property must be your principal residence, and you must have occupied it for the last three out of five years.

Question: What if I have only owned the property for three years, but during that time I took a couple of vacations? I even rented it out one summer for a few weeks while I was on vacation. Since I didn't occupy the property for the full time, technically speaking, can I still qualify for the exclusion?

Answer: Generally speaking, yes. Renting out your home for a few weeks while you were on vacation does not mean you weren't occupying for this rule.

Question: What if I took a sabbatical for a year and lived elsewhere?

Answer: Generally speaking, you could not claim that year as time during which you occupied the property. The rule seems to be that if you're away for more than a month or two you "break the chain" of occupancy.

Question: What if I owned the property for three out of the past five years, but didn't occupy it continuously. For example, for two years I treated is a rental property.

Answer: The answer is that you get the exclusion as long as you occupied the property for 36 full months, regardless if that time was continuous or intermittent.

Question: What if I have been living in a condo for the past three out of five years? Does that qualify as a principal residence?

Answer: Yes. Many types of homes qualify, including a stock cooperative and a mobile home. In some cases even yachts used as houseboats have qualified.

While these are the main rules regarding the exclusion, there are some other interesting questions that also arise. They include the following:

Question: Can I revoke the exclusion?

Answer: Yes, for example, if you later marry and want to claim it with your new spouse, you can revoke the earlier exclusion. The time limit for this is presumably three years, the time you have to file an amendment to your tax return. Also, you would have to pay the taxes you didn't have to pay previously, as well as the interest.

Question: Can the exclusion be combined with deferral?

Answer: This is a most interesting question since it suggests excellent tax planning ideas. In general, you can combine the exclusion with deferral of income on a principal residence. Thus, you can sell your current expensive home, take out much of the cash without paying taxes on it, and then buy a smaller, less expensive home, deferring some of your equity to that next home. Let's take an example:

Combining Exclusion With Deferral

1. Calculating the adjusted sales price

Sales price of your current home	$ 200,000
Exclusion	−125,000
Adjusted sales price	$ 75,000

2. Calculating the taxable gain

Price of your new home '	$ −60,000
Taxable gain	$ 15,000

3. Calculating the total gain

Sales price of your current home	$ 200,000
Basis	$ 50,000
Total	$ 150,000

(We're assuming that your basis in the old home is roughly $50,000—see how to calculate this in the last chapter.)

4. Calculating the deferral

Price of new home		$ 60,000
Total gain	$ 150,000	
Exclusion	−125,000	
Taxable gain	−15,000	
	$ 10,000	$ −10,000
Adjusted (new) basis of new home		$ 50,000

While the calculations may seem complex, they are actually quite logical. You're allowed to exclude $125,000. Since the new home you bought (in our example) cost less than the adjusted sales price of your old (after the exclusion), you must pay tax on the difference [2]. The remainder of the gain, is deferred to your new home [4].

Note that had you not bought a new home and deferred $10,000 of gain to that home, you would have had to pay tax on that $10,000 in the year of the sale. Or, if the new home you bought had cost more money, you might have been able to defer the entire gain.

Exclusion Without Deferral

Sales price of your current home	$ 200,000
Exclusion	−125,000
Adjusted sales price	$ 75,000
Less basis	$ −50,000
Taxable gain	$ 25,000

Comparison of Exclusion With and Without Deferral

Taxable gain without deferral	$ 25,000
Taxable gain with deferral	$−15,000
Amount deferred	$ 10,000

In this example you avoided paying taxes on $10,000 of gain by combining it with the exclusion and deferring it to the purchase of a new home.

Tip

Note that the exclusion rule does not require you to choose it when you are 55 years old. You can wait. This allows you to plan ahead and take it at the most opportune time. (Keep in mind, however, that the government both giveth and taketh away. If you choose to wait and at some time in the future the government decides to do away with the exclusion, you could lose out.)

Remember, the rule gives you an exclusion of *up to* $125,000. If you do not take the whole amount, you lose the difference. Thus you may want to wait until you have enough gain (deferred or otherwise) in your home to take full advantage of it.

15

Buying Your Next Home Before You Sell

A few years ago I was selling my own home. I had listed it and anticipated a fairly quick sale. As soon as the sign went up on my front lawn, I began looking for a new house. To my surprise, I found the ideal next home within a week.

Now I was faced with a dilemma. I had found the house that I wanted. Yet, I couldn't buy because I hadn't yet sold my old house...and I was counting on using the money from my old house to purchase the new one. What was I to do?

This problem is faced by many sellers. How you resolve it determines whether you get the next house you want, whether you sell your present house for a good price, and whether or not you get to sleep well while the whole thing sorts itself out.

Buying on a Contingency

In my case I purchased the new home on a contingency. Contingencies were discussed in an earlier chapter from the perspective of the seller. Now you get a chance to look at them from the perspective of the buyer.

My offer to the sellers was simply that I would buy the house subject to the sale of my present house. In all other ways the offer I made them, including a reduced price and terms in my favor, was the same as if I was coming in as a cash buyer.

However, the sellers were not fools. They realized that if they accepted my offer, they would be tying up their home subject to the sale of my home. In other words, instead of just having to worry about selling their own home, they had to worry about mine being sold as well.

At first they wanted to reject the offer; however, the market at the time, though warm, was not hot, and this was the first offer they had. So they agreed. However, they demanded a higher price, slightly better terms, and they put a time clause into the contingency. I had 30 days in which to sell my house.

I didn't mind the 30 day clause, since I felt my present house was priced right for a quick sale. However, I didn't like paying a higher price or getting less favorable terms. Yet, I wanted this new house and I realized I was in a weak bargaining position. So I accepted.

Trap

If you buy contingent on the sale of your present home, beware of the pressures it puts on you to sell. You may want the new home so badly that you reduce the sales price of your current home and accept less than you otherwise would. It may be better to simply lose the next house than to take too little for your present one.

Tip

If you buy a new home contingent on the sale of your old one, be sure that the contingency clause states that if you cannot sell your present home within the agreed upon time, you are released from the purchase of the new home and your deposit is fully refunded. If you do not state this, should your present home not sell, you might still be liable to purchase the new or you might lose your deposit.

As luck would have it, I found a buyer for my old home within a week. The buyer fell in love with the place and offered within a few thousand dollars of my asking price. I accepted the offer.

Now, I was involved in two deals. On the one hand, I was selling my present home. On the other, I was purchasing another home.

As part of the sales agreement on the purchase of my new home, I had stipulated that once I found a buyer for my old home, I would have 60 days to close escrow. As soon as I informed the sellers of my next home that I had found a buyer, that 60-day period began to run.

Problems With Contingency Deals

It should have been a smooth deal. The buyers of my home should have quickly qualified for a loan and made the purchase. I would then have my equity out, and I could purchase the next home.

That, however, wasn't the way it went. The new buyers of my old home had some credit problems. They tried lender after lender only to be turned down each time. Soon, 45 days had gone by, and they still hadn't found a new loan.

I contacted the sellers of my next home and asked for an extension, explaining the circumstances. They refused. Although they had agreed to sell to me, they had kept the house on the market, and they had several other interested buyers. If I couldn't complete the sale within the agreed upon 60-day period, they would gladly refund my deposit and sell to one of the other buyers. I was between a rock and a hard place.

Fifty-five days into the deal, the agent for the sellers of my new home came to me and said that either I had to "bite the bullet" or forget the deal.

My options were these:

1. I could simply back out of the purchase of the new home. My sales agreement allowed me to get my full deposit back.

2. I could proceed with the purchase of the new home. However, I would have to borrow extra money to do this.

3. If I proceeded with the purchase and then my old house didn't sell, I'd have two houses and two mortgages on which I'd have to pay.

Buying With a Bridge Loan

I opted to go ahead with the purchase of the new home. I went to a savings and loan association and explained my predicament. I said I wanted a short-term loan based on the equity of my old house. The money would be used for the down payment of the new home. This is called "bridge" financing.

The lender agreed. I would be charged a fairly high interest rate. However, since the loan would, presumably, only be for a few months at most, the total cost wouldn't be that high.

I got the money, used it as a down payment, and completed the purchase of my new home within the 60 day period. Now I had two houses and three loans—the mortgage on each home plus the bridge loan.

___

Don't think that you can recoup some of your expenses by renting out one of the properties. If the deal for the old home goes through, there are only a few weeks or months at the most involved—not enough time to interest a good tenant. In the example just mentioned, it was also not feasible to rent out the new home because if the sale of the old one suddenly went through, I'd need to move immediately. You're stuck paying on two houses.

In my case things turned out fine. Eventually, the buyers for my old house were able to find a lender, they got their loan, paid me my money, and moved in. I paid off the bridge loan and had successfully purchased a new home before selling my old one.

Trap
___

Sometimes it won't work. Sometimes you won't be able to sell your old home quickly, or for that matter, at all. You must, therefore, be prepared to carry the mortgages on two properties. If you can't do this, it's dangerous to become involved in bridge financing or in buying before you sell.

Other Alternatives

There have been times in real estate, particularly when interest rates are high and it's difficult to sell homes, that buying before selling assumes staggering proportions. I can recall one particular deal in which there were seven sellers, all buying new homes on related contingency agreements.

Seller A agreed to buy seller B's home contingent on the sale of his own. Seller B then went out and bought seller C's home contingent on the sale of his own. Seller C went out and did the same thing. Seven sellers in a row, all trying to play musical chairs with their houses. Ultimately, it all came down to seller A. If his buyers didn't qualify, he could not purchase home B. Then B couldn't purchase home C, and so forth. One loan refused, and the whole game would come to an abrupt halt.

Yes, such strange deals do occur, and surprisingly, more often than not they go through. However, to avoid getting caught in such entanglements, here are some alternatives:

1. Wait. Don't make a commitment on your next home at least until you've got a buyer and a signed sales agreement on your current house. At least that way, you'll be in a better bargaining position with the seller of your next home, and you'll feel more secure that the deal will go through.

2. Consider renting. Sell your present home and then rent. Give yourself the time to look for just the right home. Put the money in the bank and earn interest on it. Remember, you have up to two years to roll over your gain before you must pay taxes on it.

3. If you do buy contingent on the sale of your old home, try to avoid having a time clause inserted. It's rare that sellers won't insist on this, but if you can avoid getting it inserted, you then have plenty of time to sell your present home. If the sellers do insist on a time clause, try to get it for as long as possible into the future.

4. If you must get a bridge loan, build in as many protections as possible. Try to get a loan that can be converted to a permanent, long-term loan in case you can't sell your present home. Try to get a loan with as low monthly payments as possible. And shop around for the lowest interest rate. Today, many lenders offer bridge financing.

5. Consider a "guaranteed" sale. If you buy a new home contingent on the sale of your present one, some real estate offices, in order to make deals, will guarantee to purchase your present home if it doesn't sell within a set period of time. This guarantee may allow you to sleep easier and can make the difference between a quick deal and one that drags on for a long period of time.

Trap

Many of the so-called "guarantees" that agents sometimes make are not really to your advantage. For example, be sure that the sales price the agent is willing to pay is, in fact, the market price. Sometimes the guarantees will offer to buy the home from you, but at a reduced price.

Also, be sure that the guaranteed sale is just that. Be sure that the agent agrees to actually buy your old home, not simply to arrange bridge financing for you and then keep it on the market. You can do the latter for yourself. You want the agent to take over title and to pay off your equity. In other words, you want to be out of the property and not have it still hanging on as a potential headache.

See a further discussion of guaranteed sales in the chapter on listings.

In today's real estate market with housing prices so high, over 80 percent of all buyers must sell their present home in order to be able to afford their next home. This means that your chances of wanting to buy before you sell are very high. Don't be afraid to do it. Many people, including your author, have done it many times and quite successfully. Just be sure that you protect yourself at all times.

16

Selling a Condo
or Co-op

If the home you want to sell is a condominium or a stock cooperative, you may have some special concerns. Marketing the property may be a problem as may be getting the approval of other owners. We'll look into the special situation of condominium and stock cooperative sellers in this chapter.

Selling a Condo

Selling a condo is virtually identical to selling a single-family home in terms of the procedure followed. There are, however, several problems that occur which are unique to the group living situation of condominiums.

Market

It's important to understand that the market for condominiums is considerably different from the market for single family homes. For whatever reason, condominiums, with certain exceptions, have been looked upon as somewhat less desirable homes. As a result, for a given amount of square footage, condos have generally sold for less than single-family homes.

In addition, as soon as you put your condo on the market, you are sure to realize that the appreciation is lower as well. A close friend recently sold his condo in the San Jose, California area and was shocked to discover that, after holding it for four years, he only had a 20 percent price appreciation. During that same time, houses in his area showed a nearly 50 percent price appreciation.

Trap

When you buy a condo, you generally pay less than you would for a detached home. This is one of the reasons many people opt for condos. However, when you sell you generally receive less as well.

Finally, condos tend to be the last properties sold. In a warm or cool market it's going to take longer to sell a condo, in general, than it will to sell a single-family home. Even in a hot market, condos usually don't go as fast.

There is an important exception here, and that's for condos which have extraordinary locations. Some condominiums in Manhattan, for example, or in downtown Chicago, or even in parts of Los Angeles have seen soaring prices and incredible appreciation. There are a number of probable reasons for this.

In high density areas, condos may be the only private residences available. Also, since many urban condos offer guarded entrances, they may afford a degree of safety not available in private homes—a big consideration in downtown areas. Finally, those who buy condos in these areas may be individuals or couples who are "empty nesters" and who don't want to be bothered with the upkeep that comes with maintaining a detached home.

Other than this exception, however, when you sell your condo, you should generally not anticipate receiving the much higher price appreciation that houses may have shown in your area. In order to sell you're going to have to find a buyer who wants the particular amenities that condo life offers. In other words, you're going to have to find a buyer much like yourself (at least as you were when you bought).

Advertising

Another problem with selling the condominium has to do with letting others know it's for sale. With a single family home, one of the best (if not the best) methods of advertising is to put a "For Sale" sign in the front yard. Since the front yard of a condo is commonly owned, you normally can't do that. Most condominium bylaws, in fact, preclude your putting a "For Sale" sign for your condo in any common areas and may, in fact, prohibit you from even putting such a sign on the exterior walls, doors, or in the window of your own unit.

Thus letting people know that you have a condo for sale can be difficult. For this reason I always suggest that condo owners seriously consider using real estate agents. Agents have buyers who are specifically looking for condo units and can bring them by your unit.

Alternately, if you decide to sell FSBO, my suggestion is to try advertising heavily in the local papers. This doesn't necessarily mean a larger ad than suggested in an earlier chapter, but rather steady advertising. Without a sign in front, you can only attract buyers through other, usually more expensive, ads.

Tip

If you advertise your condo, you may have some trouble giving a buyer instructions on getting there. Some condominiums are large developments and it can be easy to get lost trying to find a particular unit. Buyers may simply not be willing to expend the effort necessary to find your unit and, after a few tries, may give up. Therefore, why not meet the potential buyer at some commonly known location such as a nearby restaurant, landmark, or even the front of the development. Then you can bring the buyer into your unit.

Stock Cooperatives

Co-ops can have all of the problems associated with selling condos as earlier described. However, in general, co-ops have been limited to the east coast and have usually been built in high-density areas, as opposed to condos which have been built right next to single-family developments across the country. As a result, they do not usually have the reputation for slow appreciation that condos do. Many of the co-ops in Manhattan, for example, have shown the strongest appreciation of any residential units in the city.

Co-ops, however, can have an additional problem that condos usually do not have. That relates to getting the approval of the current owners for your buyer. When you own a condo, you normally have fee simple title. That's the same sort of title that you have when you own a single family home. Thus, when you sell, you transfer title to your property via a deed, and the other owners in the condominium development may have no say about the sale.

With a co-op, however, you generally have ownership in the form of stock shares. You transfer ownership by selling your shares of stock to the new buyers.

However, the procedure may involve turning your shares in to the co-op management and having them issue new shares to the buyers. Along the way, depending on how the articles of incorporation or the bylaws are written, the directors of the co-op may have some say as to who buys your property. That is, they may have the right to refuse to issue stock to the new purchaser, thus effectively tying up your sale.

This control is, in fact, one of the factors that may make your co-op more valuable and desirable. Many buyers like being able to have some control over who their neighbors will be.

Of course, such control is more limited today than it was in the past. In general, co-ops may not limit buyers in terms of race, religion, or national origin. However, in recent years some exclusive co-ops have attempted to restrict buyers in terms of their income levels, their occupations, or even the size of their families.

When you go to sell, be sure you check to see what restrictions, if any, apply in your case. While you could certainly fight such restrictions, you're more likely to accomplish your goal of selling quickly if you find out the rules and then find a buyer who qualifies.

17
Conclusion

Selling your home can be a long, drawn out, and traumatic experience, or it can be quick and easy. A lot depends on factors beyond your control such as market conditions and the location of your property. However, how well or badly the sale goes also depends to a large degree on your own state of mind.

The key word is "expectations."

After reading this book you should have an excellent idea of what to expect. You should know how to determine price, how to prepare your property for sale, how to find an agent (or sell FSBO), how to negotiate with buyers, even what to do when your property doesn't sell. In other words, you should have a realistic idea of what you can expect.

One final word of advice, however. Be aware that no two sales, no two deals, are exactly the same. As prepared as you may be, when you go to sell, something totally unexpected may occur. Every time I sell a property, I know that in the back of my mind I'm wondering, how's it going to turn out this time?

When the unexpected does happen, the best advice is to flow with it. You can't plan for the unexpected, but you can react quickly. When you need specific advice, don't hesitate to consult with:

An agent—Most will consult with you at no charge, and because of their knowledge of the market, they may be able to provide a ready solution to whatever your problem is.

An attorney—Be sure your select one who specializes in real estate. The first consultation should be free because that's when you state your problem to see if the attorney can help you with it. In general, fees for real estate problems, unless the problems are unusual, tend to be fairly low.

An accountant or tax planner—Check with one *before* you make a move that has tax consequences. Tax planning is far less expensive and far more effective than later trying to cure a tax problem.

An escrow officer—This person can often give you excellent advice and help regarding the procedure to be followed in closing a deal as well as in preparing any documents you need.

A mortgage banker—They are listed under this heading in the phone book and can provide you with up-to-date information on mortgages in your area. Also check with loan officers at savings and loan associations.

The state real estate regulatory agency—They go by many different names such as the Department of Real Estate, Real Estate Commission, Director of Real Estate, Division of Licensing, Department of Licensing and Regulation, and so forth. They are usually located in the state capital, and a quick call to a local agent can get you the correct name and probably even a phone number. If you have any problems with an agent don't hesitate to call. They may also be able to help in other areas of a transaction.

In addition, there are many fine books on virtually every aspect of real estate located in your public library.

Trap

In recent years there has been a spate of "get rich quick in real estate" books, many of which espouse unwise, even dangerous tactics. These can usually be identified by their promise that if you follow what they say, with little to no effort you can become as wealthy as Midas. Beware of these books and their schemes. As W.C. Fields used to say, "You can't cheat an honest man." A good deal is one in which both you and the buyer profit. Look for a win/win sale and you won't lose.

Index

About the Author

Robert Irwin has been a successful real estate broker for over 25 years and has helped buyers and sellers alike through every kind of real estate transaction imaginable. He has been a consultant to lenders, investors, and other brokers and is one of the most knowledgeable and prolific writers in the field. His books include *Making Mortgages Work for You, How to Find Hidden Real Estate Bargains, The McGraw-Hill Real Estate Handbook, The Handbook of Property Management,* and *Finding and Managing Profitable Properties.* His latest book, *Tips and Traps When Buying a Home,* will also be of great interest to you if you are planning to buy a new house at the same time that you dispose of the house you currently own.